Active Science 3

**Richard Gott
Gareth Price
Tony Thornley**

CollinsEducational

An imprint of HarperCollinsPublishers

Collins Educational, 77–85 Fulham Palace Road, London
W6 8JB

First published 1991

ISBN 0 00 327465 9

Authors' acknowledgements

The first draft of Chapter 13 was written by Chris King.
The authors would also like to thank Kevin Flint and Phil
Sanderson for ideas which have been used in *Active
Science 3*.

Photograph acknowledgements

The authors and publishers are grateful to the following for
permission to reproduce photographs on the pages indicated.
(T = top, B = bottom, M = middle, L = left, R = right)

Aerofilms Ltd   17T
Allsport   37, 68T
Ancient Art & Architecture Collection   6BR, 25
Patrick Bailey   17R
Barnaby's Picture Library   58T, 90T
Bernstein Group plc   54M
Bridgeman Art Library   139
John Birdsall Photography   50, 62B
British Aerospace/Davis Gibson Advertising   60R
The Old Bushmills Distillery Co Ltd   73
J Allan Cash Ltd   20B, 62L, 81B, 105
Christie's   10T
Bruce Coleman Ltd   40L, 95L, 100L
Herman Kokojan/Black Star/Colorific!   112B
Derrick Warner/Edinburgh Photographic Library   54T
ECC Group   102L
Mark Edwards/Still Pictures   9BR, 94L&BR
Vivien Fifield Picture Library   143
Forestry Commission   101BL
Galvanizers' Association   60R
GAMMA   107
GeoScience Features Picture Library   7TL, TM, M, MR, BM,
   10B, 11TL, TM, TR, ML, MR, BL, BR, 14MR
Adam Ginalski   18BR
Sally & Richard Greenhill   115T
Holt Studios   95B
Hulton-Deutsch   58B
Mike Hoggett/ICCE   8M
Daisy Blow/ICCE   51L
Icelandic Photo & Press Service   24B
Ilford Ltd   72
Impact/Andrew Moore   26R, John Arthur   42B, 102R, Mark
   Cator   101TR, 110B, Christopher Pillitz   110L, Homer
   Sykes   111R, 111B
Kemira Fertilisers   66B
Frank Lane Picture Agency Ltd   15BR
Landform Slides   9ML, 15ML, 16B, 20TR
London Fan Company   77
Fiona Marsh   30TL, 35T&M

John Mills Photography   103
NASA   130TL
NASA/Jet Propulsion Laboratory   133BR, 134, 135T
NHPA/Henry Ausloos   32R, Manfred Danegger   95T,
   J Habl   101TL, Roger Tidman   101M, Michael Leach   108L
National Anti-Vivisection Society   40T
Nature Conservancy Council   100R
Network Photographers   110M&L, 112T
United Kingdon Nirex Ltd   26L
Nuclear Electric plc   27B
Omicrom Vakuumphysik GMbH   56T
Robert Opie Collection   104
Oxford Scientific Films   22R, 30TR, 34TL, 94TR, 95M&R, 100M
Planet Earth   14T, 30B, 31, 32L, 34MR&B, 35R
Gareth Price   8R, 10M, 18B, 22L, 29L&M, 40B, 41, 42T, 48B, 49,
   51R, 53, 56L,M&R, 57TR&BR, 59M&TL, 60T, 62M, 65R, 74, 80,
   81T, 86, 88, 90B, 91, 108R, 114B, 115M, 116, 120T, 124
Rothampstead Experimental Station   66TR
Royal National Institute for the Deaf   120
Science Museum   138
Science Photo Library   14ML, BL, 14/15, 45, 46, 57MT, 58R, 59B,
   66TL, 89, 114T, 118, 119, 123, 126, 129, 130M&B, 133TM&L,
   135B, 136, 137
Society for Cultural Relations with the USSR   128
Roger Scruton   6BL
Skyscan Balloon Photography   6M
Michael Spincer   75
Tony Stone Worldwide   38, 62R
Syndication International   48T
Thomas Tait & Sons Ltd   101BR
Charles Tait   6T
C & S Thompson   18T, 54B, 66M, 70, 93, 106, 120B
Thorn Lighting Ltd   57L
US Geological Survey   23, 24T, 29R
Tony Waltham   7TR, ML, BL, BR, 8L, 9M, TR, BL, 11M, BM, 12,
   14BR, 15TR, 19M, 20TL, 97, 102T
ZEFA   19T, 58L

Cover
Clockwise from top right: Tony Stone Worldwide, Oxford
Scientific Films, Tony Stone Worldwide, Laura Friar, NASA/Jet
Propulsion Laboratory.

Designed by Wendi Watson
Edited by Michael Spincer
Picture research by Caroline Thompson

Artwork by John Booth, Jerry Collins, Gay Galsworthy,
Cedric Knight, Sally Neave, PanTek Arts, Kate Shannon
Darby and Marion Tasker.

Typeset by Dorchester Typesetting Group Ltd

Printed and bound by Cambus Litho, East Kilbride

Illustration acknowledgements

The authors and publishers are grateful to the following for
permission to reproduce adaptations of illustrations on the
pages indicated.

Baillière Tindall   38T
The *Guardian*   113B
Scientific American   113M&B

Contents

What it takes for you to be good at science

There are five areas you need to cover to be good at science.

Communicating and interpreting

Communicating

You should be able to:

- read tables, pie charts, bar charts and line graphs and know what they mean.
- pick out important pieces of information from books, magazines and worksheets.
- find patterns in tables, pie charts, bar charts and line graphs.
- describe clearly an experiment you have done.

Observing

Observing

You should be able to:

- pick out the important things about an object (and ignore other things).
- find similarities in a group of objects.
- find differences among the objects in a group.

Planning investigations

Planning

You should be able to:

- design an investigation to solve a problem.
- decide what equipment to use.
- decide what measurements to take.
- decide how the results would give an answer to the problem.

Investigating and making

Investigating

You should be able to:

- decide what a problem means and how to solve it.
- set up and try out suitable apparatus.
- alter the investigation if it does not give an answer to the problem.
- use the results to work out an answer.
- decide when you need to do more experiments to check your results.

Basic skills

Basic skills

You should be able to:

- make tables of results.
- draw pie charts, bar charts and line graphs.
- know when to use each type of graph or chart.
- read measuring instruments as accurately as necessary.
- follow instructions for doing experiments.

You will get plenty of chances to practise these skills. Each chance for testing a skill is marked in this book with a coloured box.

$\boxed{W}$ means there is a worksheet to go with the topic.

Safety

You will find these signs used in the book. This is what they mean:

DANGER

This sign is warning you that there are hazards here. You must take great care.

EYE PROTECTION MUST BE WORN

This sign tells you that you must protect your eyes by wearing special glasses.

TOXIC

This sign warns you that you are using or making something poisonous.

In *Active Science* you explore science. Often, you plan your own investigations, and we cannot give you detailed instructions in the book. So you must think about safety for yourself.

Always include safety in your plans for investigations.
Always get your teacher to check your plans before you carry them out.
Always pay attention to the hazard warnings in this book.
Always follow safety rules.

Always think safe!

13 THE EARTH
13·1 Building with stones

For thousands of years, people have used rocks and stones for building. The photographs on this page show some examples.

1 What are the advantages of using rocks and stones?

2 What are the disadvantages?

● Make a list of the materials used to make your own home.

3 Which of these materials are naturally occurring stones?

4 Which have been made by human beings?

Some of the stones used to build Stonehenge came from the west coast of Wales. This is over 150 kilometres from Salisbury Plain.

5 Why did the builders fetch stones from such a long way away?

Salisbury Plain, Wiltshire: ▶
Stonehenge was built over 3000 years ago

Building a modern dry-stone wall: Deirdre Patten is the first woman to become a Master Craftsman of the Dry Stone Walling Association ▼

▲ *Orkneys: old house built from beach stones*

Machu Picchu, Peru: this wall was built by the Incas whose empire lasted from AD 1100 to about AD 1500. The stones fit together perfectly without mortar ▼

Bricks

If the local materials are not suitable for building, people have tried to improve them. Bricks are the best example of this. They are made all over the world. Clay is made into lumps that are the right size and shape for building. In some countries bricks are also baked (or fired in a kiln).

Testing bricks ⚠ 😎 W̶

● Make some bricks. Then test them for strength. Investigate one of the questions below. Get your plans checked by your teacher first.

6 Which are stronger: bricks that have been fired or bricks that have not?

7 How does the amount of water used affect the strength of the finished brick?

8 Which is more important for strong bricks:
   – the amount of water in the original mix
   – the time spent in the kiln

9 What other things could affect the strength of bricks? If possible, test your ideas.

Sorting rocks W̶

Look closely at these rocks. Sort them into two or three groups.

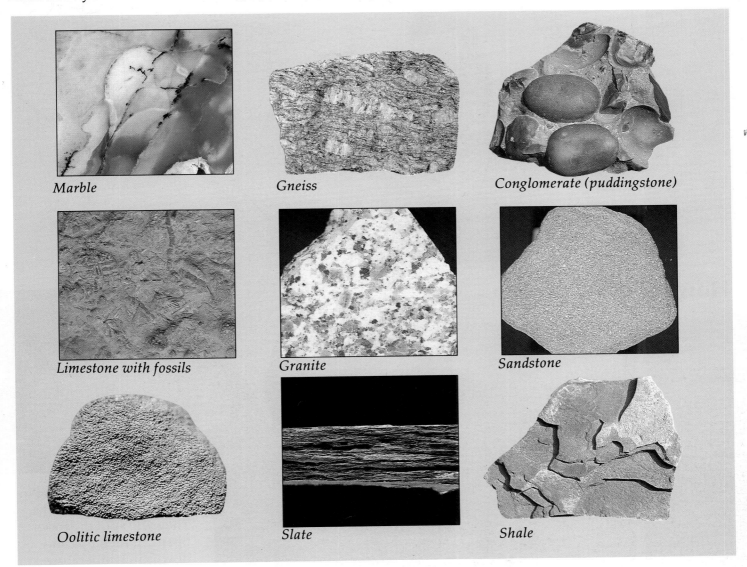

Marble

Gneiss

Conglomerate (puddingstone)

Limestone with fossils

Granite

Sandstone

Oolitic limestone

Slate

Shale

EXTRAS

1 Make a list of building materials. Give a use for each one and then explain why it is used. For example, why are certain types of materials used for motorways and others for building walls?

2 Birds are good builders. Some fish also build nests. What other types of animals build homes? Why do they do this? What problems do these animal builders face? How do they solve them?

13·2 Breaking rocks

A rock-breaking machine ⚠️ 😎

Rocks do not last for ever. Even large boulders can eventually be broken down to fine sand. If the sand is mixed with organic material, soil can be made. This takes a very long time. Only a few centimetres of soil are made in a hundred years.

● Design and build a machine to break rocks. Your machine should let you compare the strengths of different rocks.

How rocks are broken

The sea has washed away this cliff.

1 What will happen next?
2 How can we stop it happening?

Acid rain has dissolved away this statue.

3 How can we stop it getting worse?

Ice crystals are growing in the cracks in these rocks. They will split the rocks open. Sudden ups and downs in temperature cause more damage than permanent freezing.

4 Why?
5 How can buildings made of rock be protected from ice shattering?

Rock attack

Look at the rocks, stones and other building materials round your school and home. Are there any signs that these materials are being attacked (weathered)? For each material:

6 Look carefully at the surface. Is it soft? How can you tell? Are all the surfaces the same?

7 Have the surfaces changed colour?

8 Are the surfaces covered in lichen or moss? Are all the surfaces covered? Gently lift some of the lichen or moss. Are any bits stuck to the roots? Put the mosses or lichens back and pat them down.

9 Are the materials cracked? How many and what sort of cracks can you see?

Give each material a number on a scale from 6 (badly weathered) to 1 (hardly weathered at all).
Use your results to answer these questions.

10 Which types of rocks are most easily damaged?

11 Which types last longest?

12 Which parts of a building need the strongest rock?

13 Which parts could be made of softer, cheaper rocks?

Weathering and erosion

Rocks are broken into smaller pieces by the things round them. This is called weathering. If these broken rocks are also moved away, it is called erosion. Think about your work on rocks and look at the photos here.

● Make a list of all the things you can think of that break down (weather) rocks.

● Make a list of all the things you can think of that can erode rocks (move the broken pieces away).

EXTRAS

1 Why are pebbles on the beach often smooth and round?

2 Design a large-scale rock crusher. Your design should include a way of grading the crushed rock into piles of different-sized lumps.

3 Screes are piles of loose, weathered rocks found under cliffs in mountain areas. Why should you not walk on screes?

13·3 Minerals and gems

A mineral is a chemical found in a rock. Sometimes rocks are made up of a mixture of different minerals. Minerals that are precious are called gems. Gems can be polished and cut to make jewels.

1 Look at the photos opposite. What is it that makes a mineral precious ?

Expensive gems are cut and polished to be used in jewellery. Less precious gems are only polished.

Polishing stones

● Make a machine to round and polish rough stones. You will be able to use abrasive powder in your machine to help the grinding down. You can use shaking, rolling or rotating methods. You will need to think about:

– how much shaking, rolling or rotating you will need,
– how you will make a machine that works for a long time.

● Use your machine to investigate these problems:

2 How does the hardness of the minerals affect how long they need to be in the polisher?

3 Which speeds up the polishing of the stones more:
– speeding up the rate of movement of the machine?
– changing the quality of abrasive powder?

4 What else could affect how easily gems are polished?

£4 million worth of rock!

A few pounds' worth of rock

Native silver

Gems in the rock

Gems are crystals. Some gems are found in mineral veins. These form when hot water from deep in the Earth flows up through cracks in the rock. The water contains dissolved minerals. As the water rises it cools and crystals of the minerals grow along the sides of the cracks.

Nuggets of precious metals like gold and silver can form in this way too.

Some gem crystals are made out of liquid rock as the rock cools down and becomes solid. Other gems form in rocks that are changed by heat and pressure.

Identifying minerals

- Make a key for identifying minerals, such as those below.
- Use your key to identify the minerals you are given.
- Can you find any valuable minerals near your home?

Quartz

Feldspar

Fluorite

Malachite

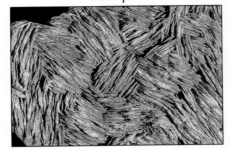

Barytes

Pyrites

Gypsum

Halite

Calcite

Hornblende

EXTRAS

1 (a) Gold is usually found in the ground as pure gold, not as a chemical compound. Why?
(b) Why was gold one of the first metals to be used by humans, even though it is so rare?

2 Use your gem polisher to find out which types of seashell stand up best to battering. Which types of shell are most likely to last longest?

3 Make a list of different gems and then do a survey to find out which are the most popular and why.

13·4 Extracting lead

Finding the lead

An ore is a rock that contains a useful metal. Unfortunately an ore usually contains a lot of other things as well. How do we get rid of the useless materials and keep the useful metal?

This mine is in the Peak District of Derbyshire. Miners dig ore from the ground. The ore contains limestone, fluorite and galena. Galena is a mineral that contains lead.

Galena

Ladywash mine, Eyam, Derbyshire

Extracting galena ⚠ 😎 ☠

How can you get rid of the limestone and fluorite in your sample? Galena is much denser than fluorite or limestone.

● The diagrams show how light and heavy particles can be separated. Try it.

1 Which works better – large or small lumps in the jigger?

2 How is the time taken to separate the mixture affected by the speed of movement of the jigger?

3 Which has more effect on the separation: the size of the particles or the speed of the jigger's movement?

Extracting the lead

1 The chemical name for galena is lead sulphide. A lead sulphide crystal is made of millions of lead and sulphur atoms held tightly together.

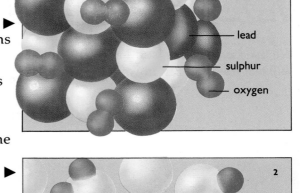

Oxygen gas is made of millions of molecules. Each of these is two atoms of oxygen joined together. At room temperature, the oxygen molecules do not affect the lead sulphide.

2 To get lead metal, the sulphur has to be removed. This is done by heating lead sulphide. The oxygen and sulphur atoms vibrate quickly when they are hot. Oxygen molecules in the air also move faster.

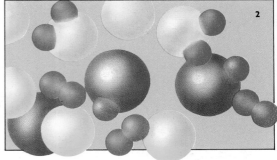

3 When the mixture is hot enough, the lead atoms split from the sulphur atoms. They join up with the oxygen atoms. This is called a chemical reaction. The reaction gives out more heat which helps more atoms to react.

lead sulphide + oxygen → lead oxide + sulphur dioxide

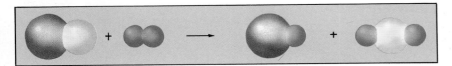

4 Next, lead has to be separated from the oxygen in lead oxide. Heating the oxide with carbon makes it react. Carbon atoms break the links between the lead and oxygen atoms. The reaction makes carbon dioxide gas. Pure lead is left behind.

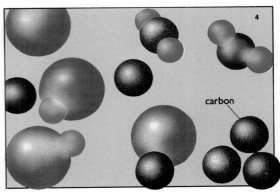

lead oxide + carbon → carbon dioxide + lead

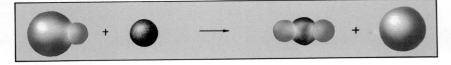

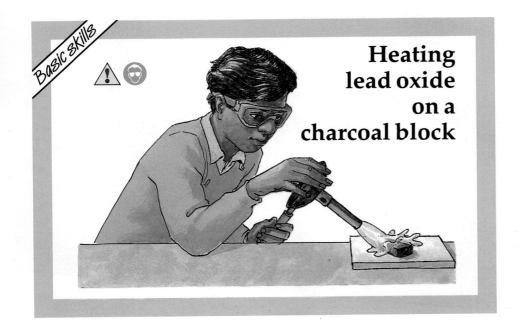

Heating lead oxide on a charcoal block

EXTRAS

1 What are some of the disadvantages of extracting metal ores from the ground? Make a list of the problems that can occur. Make another list of the uses of the metal. Can you weigh up the advantages and disadvantages? Who should do this?

2 Design a machine to sort metal scraps. It should be able to sort cheap metals like steel and iron from more expensive metals like aluminium and zinc.

13·5 Active Earth

We use sayings like 'solid as a rock' to describe something that will last for ever. But how solid are rocks? Do they last for ever?

Muddy river in Kenya

Mountain ranges in the greater Himalayas

Glaciated rocks in Greenland

The Sinai Peninsula

Fossils in limestone, Dorset

Changing rocks

Look carefully at the photographs on pages 14 and 15. They give us some information about how the rocks of the Earth are changing. Write down how they show that:
- parts of the Earth are being weathered,
- broken material can be carried away,
- the broken material can be deposited somewhere else,
- loose sand can be changed into rock,
- tremendous pressures can be produced in the Earth,
- the Earth is hot enough deep down to melt rocks,
- the Earth produces its own heat,
- parts of the Earth's surface are moving apart or together.

Lava flow from Mount Etna, Italy

A fault in sandstone, Merseyside

Sand dunes in Dyfed, Wales

EXTRAS

1 Think of places you have been to or seen on television or read about. Write a sentence about each place where:
(a) weathering of rocks is happening,
(b) sand is being carried along by water,
(c) mud is settling out of water and building up,
(d) sand or mud has been changed into rock,
(e) tremendous pressures have bent or broken layers of rock,
(f) liquid rock comes out of the ground.

2 (a) The 'active Earth' can be a problem. Where does the Earth's activity cause problems?
(b) The 'active Earth' can be very useful. How? Where is this 'activity' useful?

13·6 Sediments

Water work

Pieces of rock can be broken down in one place and then moved to another area. Sediment is made in rivers by rocks hitting against each other. The river then moves it toward the sea.

Where a river slows down, a lot of the particles it is carrying sink. This material is known as sediment. If the water is very calm this sediment forms a mud bank or a sand bank. At the mouth of the river it may form a delta. Where is the delta made in your model?

Sand is made from rocks which break off cliffs and rocky shores. These are ground together by the waves and tide. The sediment, sand and small rocks can be moved large distances by sea currents.

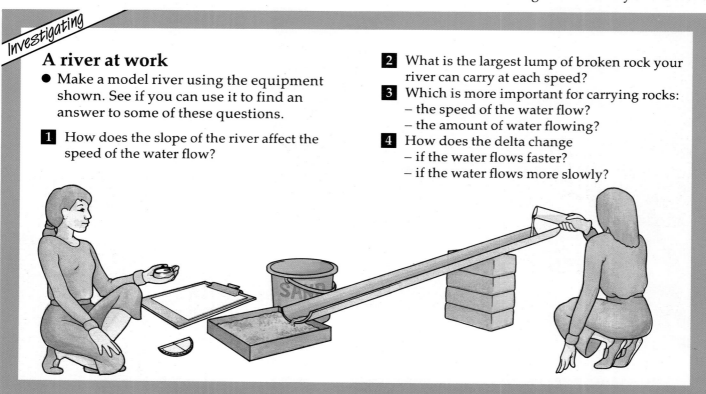

Investigating

A river at work
● Make a model river using the equipment shown. See if you can use it to find an answer to some of these questions.

1 How does the slope of the river affect the speed of the water flow?

2 What is the largest lump of broken rock your river can carry at each speed?

3 Which is more important for carrying rocks:
– the speed of the water flow?
– the amount of water flowing?

4 How does the delta change
– if the water flows faster?
– if the water flows more slowly?

Layers to landscapes

Sands, gravels and muds are laid down in layers. Over many millions of years these layers harden into rocks. These are called sedimentary rocks. Some layers may be harder than others. When rocks with hard and soft layers become worn away, the soft layers erode faster. The hard layers stick out more than the soft layers. You can see this on the photograph of a cliff in Dorset.

Hard and soft layers in the cliffs ▶
at Bridport Sands

View over the Severn Bridge area looking southwest towards Wales

How did the land form?

Look at the photograph of the Severn estuary.

● Write down as many differences as you can between areas A, B, C, and D.
● Explain how each area has formed over the years.

A *Top of sandstone cliff with good plant cover.*
B *Rocks with some seaweed growing on them.*
C *Mud with a layer of grasses and reeds.*
D *Mud flats with no plant cover.*

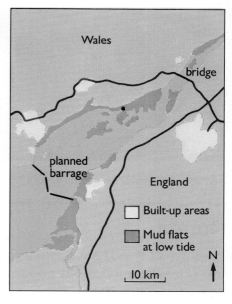

Site of the proposed Severn estuary barrage. Water flowing through turbines would generate electricity

EXTRAS

Planning

1 There are plans to build a barrage across the Severn estuary (see map). It could generate nearly 6% of all the electricity Britain needs. The barrage would be fitted with fish-passes and ship locks. It would form the biggest artificial harbour in the world. Some people say that the sediment brought down by the river will block the barrage within ten years of it being finished. Others say the barrage will be useful for fifty years. Plan an investigation to find out who is right.

2 You can make 'cakes' from sand and plaster that have soft and hard layers. Make some of these models and try to weather them with running water. Find out what landforms are made when rain and weather attack places where:
– the layers are horizontal
– the layers have been tilted so that they are vertical.

3 You have probably seen groynes (like strong wooden fences) across a beach. Why are they built? Why is the beach higher on one side than on the other? How does this help to explain what groynes do?

Groynes on a shingle beach

View of the River Wear from the footbridge in Durham

Durham

Rivers can cut through rock. It takes a very long time but water can grind away even the toughest rocks. Look at the photograph and map of Durham. A student from a local school drew the sketch map.

- Write down how the River Wear has helped to shape the land over millions of years. Use the information on this page to help you.

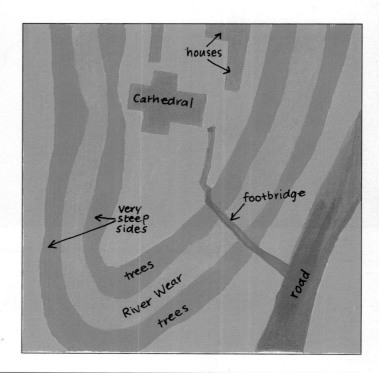

Ronda

The town of Ronda has Spain's oldest bullring. The town is built on two sides of a gorge. Only one bridge connects the two parts. A small river flows through the gorge.

▲ *General view of Ronda, Spain*

◄ *The photos on the left show houses built on the edge of the gorge and a view of the river from the bridge*

- Draw a sketch map based on the photographs of Ronda.
- Include labels which explain how the gorge has developed over the years.
- Are the houses near the edge of the gorge in any danger?

Glaciers

Glaciers are rivers of ice. They can also cut through rocks and scrape out deep valleys. About 20 000 years ago most of Britain was covered with glaciers and ice. This was the last great ice age. There had been many ice ages before then. There may be another one.

- Draw a series of four diagrams. They should show how the valley in the bottom photograph has formed from level ground. Each diagram will need to represent a different age from the Earth's history.

Aletsch Glacier, Switzerland

Nant Ffrancon, Wales, a valley formed by a glacier

EXTRAS

1 Look at the landscape round your school. Can you find any evidence of erosion? Draw maps and sketches to show what you think has happened in the past.

2 (a) What differences can you see between a valley made by a glacier and a valley made by a river?
(b) Are there any similarities?

Folding

Layers of rock were laid down by sedimentation. Forces in the Earth pushed on the layers and they crumpled up a bit like paper.

Folds in rock layers

Faulting

Part of the crust has slipped. This is known as a fault. The layers of rock have been torn and rearranged.

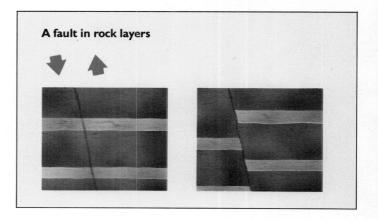

A fault in rock layers

Ingleborough

The surface of the Earth is always moving. These movements are usually too slow to see. We only see their effects in the rocks of the Earth's crust.

The photograph shows Ingleborough, a hill in Yorkshire. It has been formed over millions of years by sedimentation, folding, faulting and erosion. The drawings on the opposite page show what we think has happened.

▼ *Ingleborough, North Yorkshire*

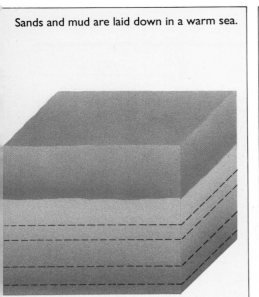

Sands and mud are laid down in a warm sea.

2 Enormous pressures form a great mountain chain.

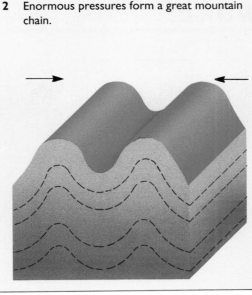

3 The mountain chain is eroded to fairly flat desert with broad rivers.

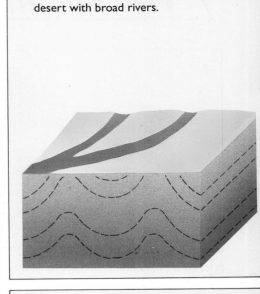

The desert is covered by sea and hundreds of metres of sediment.

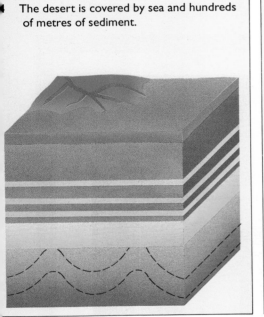

5 Sediments become rocks and the rocks become faulted.

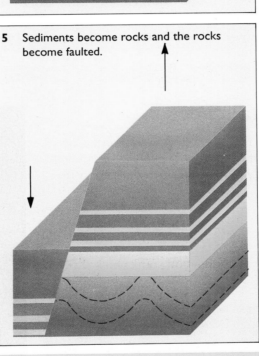

6 More erosion makes the landscape we see today.

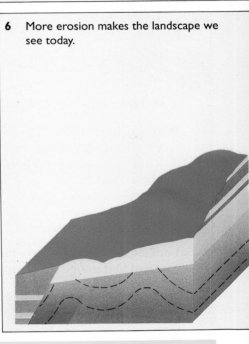

Communicating

The story of Ingleborough

- Write the story of Ingleborough. It must explain what has happened to shape the landscape and put the changes in the correct order. The drawings above will probably help you. In your account use the following words:

  – sedimentation,   – erosion,
  – folding,   – faulting,
  – weathering.

EXTRAS

1 Imagine you are looking for the remains of sea creatures. Where would you be most likely to find these? Pick a layer from the drawings on this page.

2 Write the story of the area where you live. You will need to use maps and books to find clues about what happened.

3 What will happen next to Ingleborough? Draw a seventh picture to add to the series above. Explain what you would expect to see and why.

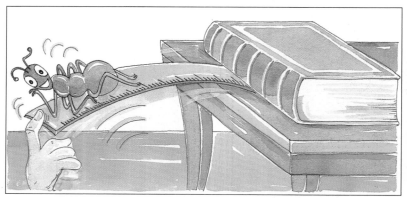

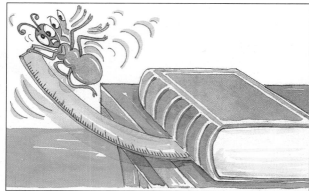

Imagine an ant sitting on the end of a ruler over the edge of a desk. It is safe while you bend it, but when you let go . . .

Earthquakes are a bit like this. The Earth's surface has cracks in it called faults. Rocks rub against each other along these faults. At first the rocks bend and stretch. In the end they can bend no further. They break and snap into new positions.

Investigating

Detecting earthquakes

Checking seismometer records in Seattle, USA

- A seismometer is a machine to detect earth movement. Can you design one? You could start with a model that can detect a vibration along a laboratory bench. You will need to think about how to:
  - make a quake,
  - detect a quake,
  - measure the quake.

Look at the pictures here. They may give you some clues. Take care not to damage the bench!

When you feel you have a good design:

- Test your seismometer. Whose is the best?
- See if the surface it is on makes any difference.

1 Do earthquake waves travel better through wood or stone?

San Francisco, California, 1906

The extracts below are from survivors of the earthquake that hit San Francisco in 1906.

> The first shock lasted over a minute and I watched my house collapse like a pack of cards.

> The gas main broke and I can remember hearing the hiss of the escaping gas just waiting for it to catch fire.

> Everywhere was shaking, I couldn't bear to look, I just closed my eyes and wanted to die.

> I think the second shock was the worst, it wasn't so big but it destroyed any hope of the whole quake being over. Even after the third shock I couldn't believe it had finished. I noticed I was holding my breath waiting for the next tremor.

> The water mains were completely broken. In some places water was spilling all over the street and in other places there was not a drop.

> The docks suffered the worst. They were built on a sort of soft clay. It just turned to liquid when the quake struck. I was glad I lived on the solid rock of the hills.

> The fires were my worst memory. They just burned on and on and we couldn't do anything to stop them. Even if the fire engines got through there was often no water. In the end they started blowing up buildings with dynamite to try to produce a firebreak.

EXTRAS

1 Design an earthquake-proof house. Use the information from this spread and your own common sense to work out the best possible structure. In your design explain exactly why you have chosen to build the house like that and what sorts of materials you would use.

Communicating

Emergency action

Imagine you are in charge of the earthquake rescue services. Write down an emergency action plan.
– What would you do?
– What equipment would you need?
– What would be the greatest dangers?

Mount St Helens: 1980 eruption

Mount Saint Helens is a volcano that erupted in May 1980. It exploded and sent large amounts of powdery ash into the air. Some of this was shot so high into the atmosphere that it was blown more than 1000 km before it fell back to the ground again. The crater left after the explosion was over 3 km wide.

Heimaey, Iceland: 1973 eruption

Iceland is a large island made up entirely of rock from volcanoes. It has many active volcanoes and some of these give out lava when they erupt. The photograph shows lava flowing.

1 What can be done to protect the town further down the mountain?

POMPEII – PRESERVED IN ASH

Old Pompeii was a pleasant Roman town in southern Italy. It had all the benefits of civilisation: a central forum, a library, public baths and toilets, even a jail and a police force.

Rising above the town was the extinct volcano Vesuvius.

However, in the space of 24 hours the whole town and many people in it were destroyed. The volcano Vesuvius was not extinct. Early on the morning of 24 August AD 79 it started to erupt. Ash was shot thousands of metres into the air and then drifted down like black snow onto the streets of Pompeii. The clouds of ash blotted out the Sun. People waking up to the sound of the volcano erupting must have thought their world was coming to an end. Within hours, the town was knee-deep in ash, with more raining down all the time.

Some rocks as large as a human fist fell from the sky. Even trying to escape

Plaster cast of a young woman buried in the ash

Communicating

Imagine you are a reporter from the *Pompeii Daily*. It is 24 August in the year AD 79. You are woke by the sound of the first volcani explosion.

The rock cycle

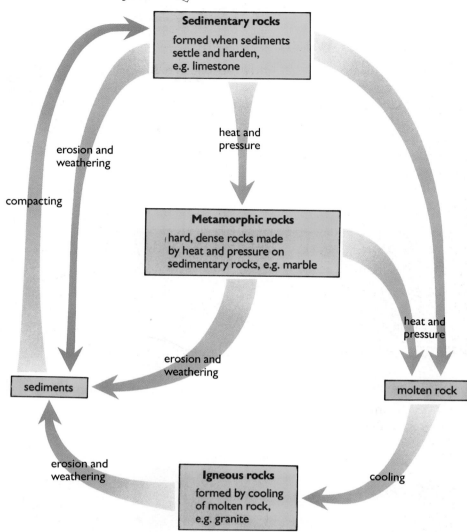

Sedimentary rocks
formed when sediments settle and harden, e.g. limestone

erosion and weathering

compacting

heat and pressure

Metamorphic rocks
hard, dense rocks made by heat and pressure on sedimentary rocks, e.g. marble

heat and pressure

erosion and weathering

sediments

molten rock

erosion and weathering

Igneous rocks
formed by cooling of molten rock, e.g. granite

cooling

Plaster cast of a watchdog caught napping

...hrough the dark and terrifying streets was ...angerous. The volcano also released ...oisonous gases containing sulphur.

...he next day the town was just a memory. ...t was completely covered in ash and had ...eased to exist.

Write a report for your paper. Use the information above and anything else you know about volcanoes to help you. Make it as realistic as you can.

In some areas of the Earth's crust, rocks are pushed underneath other rocks. These buried rocks can then be melted by the pressure and heat. The molten rocks may return to the surface in another area.

2 Where on Earth does molten rock come to the surface?
3 Why is the diagram shown called a cycle? Explain how an igneous rock could be converted through all the other types back to igneous rock again many kilometres away.

EXTRAS

1 (a) Heat some candle wax gently until it has just melted. Pour it out onto a cool surface (perhaps a microscope slide or glass tile). What shape does it make?
(b) Now try the same experiment with candle wax that is much hotter. (Be extra careful!)
(c) Use the results of your experiment to say something about how lava controls the shape of volcanoes.

2 Find out where most volcanoes and earthquakes occur. Can you explain any pattern you find?

13·11 Safe for ever?

Low-level waste

Low-level waste is only slightly radioactive. It includes used overalls, worn-out bits of reactor machinery and wrappings from more radioactive substances. Since 1959, it has been buried at Drigg in Cumbria. Workers need to use protective overalls, rubber gloves and common sense when they handle it. It can take as long as 300 years for the radioactivity to decay to safe levels.

Harmless-looking low-level waste in a double-steel container. This will now be sealed before storage

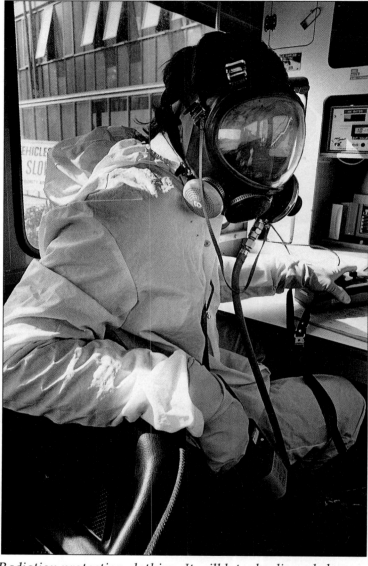

Radiation protection clothing. It will later be discarded as low-level waste

Intermediate-level waste

This is 1000 times more radioactive than low-level waste. It comes mostly from nuclear reactors. It includes metal cans that had contained nuclear fuel, bits of metalwork and various types of chemicals used in reactors. At the moment, it is produced in about twenty places round the country and is stored where it is made. It is hoped to build a disposal site for this waste where it can be dumped and left for ever. This site will be underground, possibly under the sea bed. The waste will be sealed in metal containers before dumping.

High-level waste

This is very concentrated waste produced from used fuel rods from nuclear reactors. It produces heat and has to be kept cool in a water bath. The waste will have to stay there for at least fifty years. After this, it may be made into glass blocks. These blocks will then be sealed in metal containers and dumped, probably in underground caverns. They will be radioactive for about 250 000 years. High-level waste is a very small part of the waste. However, making high-level waste produces a lot of intermediate waste as a by-product.

Which rocks are best for storing nuclear waste?

Nuclear waste must be prevented from leaking into the environment. It must be stored safely for thousands of years. Containers, that should be leak proof, have been designed and built. What could cause them to leak? The main problem is water.

Water can cause almost all metals to corrode. Some rocks allow water to pass through them easily. The water could corrode the metal waste-container and let the waste leak out. If the water rises to the surface, the danger is even greater.

The movement of water through rocks depends on two things: the porosity of the rock and the hydraulic gradient.

The porosity is a measure of the spaces between the microscopic grains that make up the rock. Rocks with large spaces (high porosity) tend to let water move easily. Rocks with a lot of cracks or faults also let the water flow easily.

The hydraulic gradient is the difference in height between where the water is coming from and where it is going. Water always flows downhill and the steeper the hill, the faster it will flow. This can be useful. A waste dump could be placed so that if a leak did occur, the water would carry the waste down through the rocks away from the surface.

1 What else could cause problems for an underground store?

The flow of groundwater through rocks

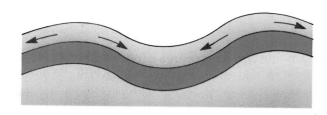

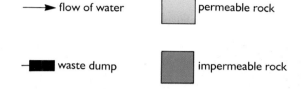

→ flow of water | ▢ permeable rock

◼— waste dump | ▢ impermeable rock

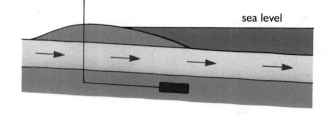

Choosing a site

● Write a report showing where the waste should be dumped. Give your reasons for choosing that particular site.

2 Where would you dump nuclear waste?
3 Where are there suitable rocks?

4 Where is most of the waste produced?
5 How easily can the waste be moved to the dump site?
6 How many people would be at risk if there was an accident?
7 Are there any areas that are particularly beautiful or easily damaged?

EXTRAS

1 What are the dangers from radioactive waste? Use your library to find out why these wastes need to be kept away from living things.

2 British Rail and the nuclear industry organised a test crash of a large train travelling at 160 km/h with a container. The engineers could not detect any cracks in the container. How useful was this test?

Crash-testing a radioactive-waste container

Planning

3 Imagine a container has leaked after it was buried. Plan an investigation to find out how fast the radioactive waste passes through rocks.

14 SURVIVAL
14·1 Dinosaurs

No one has ever seen a dinosaur, but most children know what they looked like. Almost every film about Stone Age people has a dinosaur.

1 Why is this wrong?

All we know about dinosaurs has been worked out from a few bones and teeth. Over time, these hard parts are changed into a type of rock. They end up looking almost the same as the stone where they are found. These remains are called fossils.

Careful detective work is needed to put the jigsaw together. Often bits of the jigsaw are missing but eventually it can lead to a model of the dinosaur. Comparing the model with modern animals also helps to tell us how the creatures lived. But all this is guesswork.

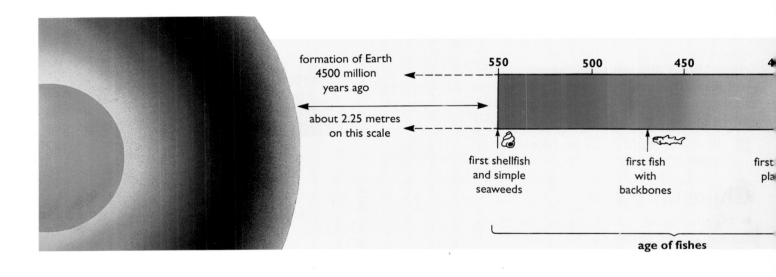

formation of Earth
4500 million
years ago

about 2.25 metres
on this scale

550   **500**   **450**   4

first shellfish
and simple
seaweeds

first fish
with
backbones

first
pla

age of fishes

This dinosaur was able to 'fly'. Enormous wings of skin stretched over its thin bones allowed it to glide through the air.

● Make a model gliding dinosaur. Find out how stable it is in the air. Can you make it fly straight for more than 3 metres?

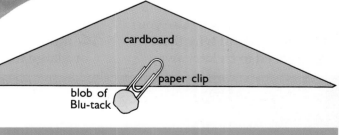

cardboard

paper clip

blob of
Blu-tack

Pterodactyl

Investigating

Investigating flight
● Which of these things are most important for a good flight:
    – bigger wings?   – a heavier head?
    – a longer body?   – a longer neck?

Fossil clues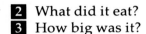

- Work out all you can about the dinosaur that left these fossils. Try to use all of the clues.

▲ *Dinosaur skull*

Apatosaurus ▶
leg bone

▲ *These are fossilised footprints. They can be made when something walks through soft mud. The mud dries and hardens. Then it sets to become a kind of fossil.*

2 What did it eat?
3 How big was it?

4 Did it walk on two or four legs?

5 Did it drag its tail on the ground or lift it in the air?

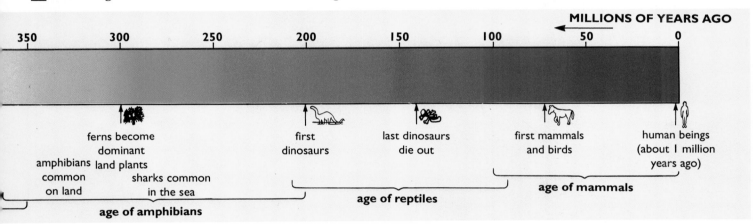

MILLIONS OF YEARS AGO

| 350 | 300 | 250 | 200 | 150 | 100 | 50 | 0 |

ferns become dominant land plants

amphibians common on land

sharks common in the sea

age of amphibians

first dinosaurs

last dinosaurs die out

age of reptiles

first mammals and birds

human beings (about 1 million years ago)

age of mammals

The end of the dinosaurs

Eventually the dinosaurs died out. By 140 million years ago only a few species remained and then these too became extinct.

What caused the dinosaurs to fail? No one is completely sure, but here are some ideas.

- There was sudden change in the climate. The dinosaurs could not cope.
- A disease appeared which wiped out the dinosaurs.

- Mammals developed which ate the dinosaurs' eggs.
- Some people say dinosaurs did not die out. They changed over many generations (evolved) into other types of animals: birds or reptiles.

- Choose the idea you think is the most likely. Write a more detailed account of the things that were happening as the dinosaurs died out.

6 What might cause the human race to die out?

EXTRAS

1 Imagine a dinosaur has been found preserved in ice and that scientists can revive it. Should they? What new ideas might we get about dinosaurs from a live one?

2 Dinosaurs left bits of teeth and bone and footprints behind. What will be left if the human race dies out? What will creatures that come after us make of these clues?

3 Can you find out about any of the more recent extinctions? What caused the dodo to die out? Or the woolly mammoth? Or the sabre-toothed tiger?

The giraffe lives in the dry grasslands of Africa. It feeds on the leaves of the few trees growing there.

Fitting in

- Make a list of the things animals need to survive.
- Make a list of the things plants need to survive.
- Look carefully at the animals and plants on these pages. Write down how each is adapted to survive.

The arrow frog is poisonous to anything that eats it.

This cactus grows in dry regions. It has no leaves and a tough, leathery skin. It only flowers once every few years – normally after a shower of rain.

The angler fish lives at the bottom of some of the deepest seas. It feeds on other fish. These are very rare at the angler fish's depth.

A coconut is actually a seed. It floats in water quite well. Coconut palms are found on almost all the islands in the southern Pacific Ocean.

The Indian tiger is one of the world's most beautiful hunters. It is almost extinct now.

Changing environments

All living things are adapted to their environments. They fit in where they live. Sometimes the environment changes and the animal has to change with it.

1. Make a list of animals that look or behave very differently in the winter and the summer. For example, a squirrel will go to sleep during the winter.
2. How do these changes help the animals to survive?
3. What changes can you notice in plants during the four seasons?

Frozen peas?

The pea seeds opposite are specially produced for growing in cold soil. The packet says they can survive frosts. The company that can produce the seeds that grow quickest in the spring will make a lot of money. Why is it useful to have seeds that can grow earlier?

Planning

- Design an investigation to find out which seeds really do stand up to frosts better.

4. What else could affect how well a pea seed germinates?

EXTRAS

1 The Kalahari Desert is one of the hottest and driest places in the world. You would not expect many animals to live there but in fact many do. 'Design' an ideal desert animal.

Show how it is adapted to its environment.

2 What are we adapted for? We cannot fly, swim very fast or run very quickly. Why are we such a successful species?

3 What difficulties will the human race face in the future? Design a new human being to survive these. Explain how your 'improved human' will solve these problems.

Plaice

Arctic fox

Camouflage

Animals which eat other animals are called predators. The animals they feed on are called prey. The predators develop better and better ways of finding and killing their prey. The prey develop better and better ways of not getting caught. Camouflage can help animals to stay alive.

Design your own camouflage markings for an animal.
● Decide where your animal is going to live and then design the best possible camouflage.
● Find some way of testing different markings to see which is most effective.

Look at the photographs on this page and in 'Staying alive 1'.

1 Why are predators in the photographs camouflaged?
2 Write down a list of the animals on this page and in 'Staying alive 1' that are predators.
3 Write down a list of the animals on this page and in 'Staying alive 1' that are prey.
4 What important differences can you find between them?

Communicating

Of mice and men . . .

Use the information on the next page to answer these questions.

5 How long did it take the people of Kern County to kill most of the predators?
6 How many acres of stubble and scattered seeds were available for the mice after the harvest?
7 How many months were the mice breeding before the cold forced them from the fields?
8 The cat is a natural predator for the mice. Why did it not solve the problem?

9 You are a reporter on the *Los Angeles Daily*. Write a report explaining why the mice were such a problem in Kern County.
10 You have been asked to judge the case of the Kern County farmers and Farm Insurance Inc. The farmers are claiming that the mice were a freak of nature and they should be compensated by the company. The insurance company say the mouse problem was created by the farmers and are refusing to pay. Explain who you think is right and why.

LOS ANGELES DAILY

Army of mice kill and eat sheep!
21 Feb 1920

Open season!
14 Mar 1910

Mayor Jim Baker today proudly announced the new vermin policy. Citizens are to be encouraged to kill as many predators as they can find. Guns and poison are to be subsidised by the state with the aim of eradicating weasels, skunks, snakes, hawks and owls within ten years.

Mouseville!
25 Jan 1920

There's a mouse in the house! There's a mouse in every house in Kern County! The cold weather has brought the mice to the towns searching for food. The only ones to benefit are the cats! One teacher found she was sharing her desk with a family of twelve mice

The Pied Piper of Kern
14 Mar 1920

Stanley Piper, a rodent officer from Washington, has declared war on an army of 100 million mice! He is expecting delivery of 40 tons of strychnine-poisoned grain by Thursday. Citizens are warned of the danger of this grain – pets and farm animals must be kept away from it.

Bumper crop
15 Sept 1919

The largest harvest ever has been recorded in Kern County. 25000 acres yielded well above average. Farmers estimate the harvest was so good many tons are left scattered on the ground by inefficient harvesting machines. Senator James Baker is said to be investigating.

Warning! Mice on Road!
5 Jan 1920

US 339 has been declared a hazard. Mice who bred in the wheat fields of Kern have been forced out by the cold snap. They have been foraging for food everywhere but when they get to the roads they end up squashed by passing cars. Police Chief Al Baker has warned 'The red road is very slippery. Drivers must take special care.'

Pet shop to close
7 Feb 1920

Mrs Edith Field is to close her pet shop in Main Street. She has been the victim of hate mail since the mouse plague started with some citizens blaming her for the invasion of mice. Mrs Field used to specialise in rare breeds of Abyssinian mice. 'I can't carry on any more' she said, 'The looks people give me make my blood run cold.'

Jim Baker is rumoured to be buying the lease and applying for permission to convert the premises into a hamburger restaurant.

Senator under investigation in poison fraud probe
29 Apr 1920

Senator Jim Baker yesterday denied the allegations that he had received payments from Kern Poisons Inc, the company selling most of the pesticides in Kern County.

EXTRAS

1 Design a 'super-efficient predator'. Explain what its prey is like. How long do you think the predator and the prey will last?

2 Sometimes we want animals to get caught. One fishing shop was selling brightly coloured maggots for bait. The owner said these attracted the fish better. Design an investigation to see if this is true.

Planning

3 Predators can detect the colour, shape and movement of their prey. Design an investigation to find out which of these three things is most important. Which gives away the prey most quickly?

14·4 Somewhere to live

In the natural world, the place where an animal lives is called its habitat. Zoos try to keep animals in conditions like their habitat. This is not always easy.

- Make a list of the things the habitat must provide for the lion.
- Do the same for all the other animals on this page.
- Design a zoo enclosure for each animal.

1 What differences are there between a zoo's habitat and the animals' natural habitats?

2 Do you think these differences make zoos cruel for animals?

3 A wolf living in Alaska would need a habitat of nearly 250 square kilometres. How can the zoo keep the wolf alive in a much smaller space?

WOLF

Wolves normally live in small family groups in the summer but will join to make a large hunting pack in the winter. They hunt deer and smaller prey in forests and remote mountain regions. The wolf is a strong runner and can travel many kilometres every day in search for food.

KILLER WHALE

The killer whales are the fiercest of all the whale species. They will attack much larger whales for food and will eat whole birds, seals and smaller porpoises. Like all whales, they normally travel in family groups and have a highly developed social life.

JELLY FISH

The large jellyfish known as a Portuguese man-of-war can be over 2 metres in length from the tip of the tentacles to the top of the body. They drift in the waters of the Atlantic Ocean. They sting and paralyse fish that swim between their tentacles. They can kill a small child and have been known to drift on to beaches in Cornwall.

LION

Lions usually live in family groups on the grassy, open plains of Africa. The female normally does the hunting and will kill wildebeest, antelope, zebra and even giraffe.

ZEBRA

Zebras normally live in herds. They feed on grass on the plains of Africa. Their stripes are very good camouflage and help to protect them from their main predators, the lions. Zebras can also run very fast if attacked.

BANDED SEA SNAKE

This snake lives its whole life in water. Its tail is flattened to act as a paddle for swimming. It feeds on fish. It lives in the warm seas from the Persian Gulf round to Japan. The banded sea snake is the most poisonous snake of all.

Energy flow

Food is one important thing provided by a habitat. Green plants are the basic food in any area. Only they are able to convert sunlight energy into food energy by photosynthesis. Green plants are called producers because they produce food from carbon dioxide and water. They use sunlight to give them the energy to do this.

Animals use plants for food. They are known as consumers because they consume food. A zebra will consume grass and use the energy in it to keep itself alive. But animals are not very good at using plant energy . Almost 90% of the energy in a plant is wasted when an animal eats it. Only about 10% of the food the animal eats is converted into 'animal'.

A lion will depend on a zebra for food. Lions cannot digest grass, so they cannot get energy from it. They kill and eat zebras. Again, most of the zebra is wasted. Only 10% of the food is used.

4 What things waste the energy going into an animal?
5 What limits the number of lions living in an area?
6 Why does a lion need a habitat of 50 square kilometres but a zebra can survive with about a fifth of a square kilometre?
7 Wildebeest, lions and zebras are all roughly the same size. Wildebeest eat grass. How many wildebeest would you expect to find in a square kilometre of grassland? Why?

Sometimes an animal will defend its habitat against other animals of the same type. A robin, for example, will try to scare off other robins that enter its habitat. A habitat that an animal defends is called its territory.

8 Why does an animal defend its territory?

EXTRAS

1 Vegetarians say that if everyone stopped eating meat there would be a lot more food to go round. Is this true? Explain your answer.

2 Dogs have territories. Think of two ways dogs show where their territories begin.

3 Factory farming is one method of producing a lot of meat from a small space. How do factory farmers make sure as much as possible of the animals' food is converted to meat? Are there any disadvantages to this?

14·5 Surviving the cold

● Write down three things in your home that help to keep you warm.

Sometimes things can go wrong. In 1987 in Britain there were 559 deaths due to hypothermia, 448 of these were old age pensioners. In the week from 16 to 23 January the temperatures were the coldest recorded this century. There were 1000 more deaths than normal. These were due to influenza, bronchitis and heart attacks as well as hypothermia.

Observing

Saving a life

It is Tuesday. The temperature outside is −4°C and Mrs Williams has not left this room for two days. Some students from the local school are looking through the window. They visit Mrs Williams every Tuesday.

● Look at the picture. Make a list of the clues that tell them Mrs Williams is in trouble.

● Write the script for a radio play (or produce your own live version on tape) that shows what happens when they knock on the door. In your play make sure you:
– warm up Mrs Williams,
– do something to make her house warmer so that this does not happen again.

Hypothermia

The normal body temperature for humans is about 37°C. This is the temperature of the core or inner parts of the body. The skin is often cooler, perhaps 34°C or 32°C.

Hypothermia can occur when the temperature of the core falls below 35°C. The first signs are feeling cold and tired. The sufferer begins to become confused and their speech may become slurred. Muscles and joints will feel stiff. As the situation gets worse, the sufferer can become so confused that they start to feel hot and take off some clothes!

Eventually people fall asleep and never wake up.

Hypothermia is particularly dangerous for old people and young babies. They cannot control their body temperature very well.

Treatment for hypothermia is to bring the body temperature slowly back to normal. Warm blankets and warm drinks help. No alcohol should be given because it makes blood rush to the skin. Why is this a bad thing?

Investigating Caving

Caving is a sport in which people often get cold and wet. Air and water deep underground are both about 4°C. The water will soon chill an unprotected caver and bring on hypothermia. In some places draughts of air can make the situation even worse.

● Pick one of the questions on the right and do an investigation to find the answer.

1 Are wet clothes better at keeping you warm than no clothes? Should you keep wet clothes on?

2 Which is more dangerous for cooling the body, wind or rain?

3 How is the cooling effect of the wind related to its strength?

4 What else can affect the speed you cool down?

EXTRAS

1 What happens to your hands in very cold weather? Can you explain what you can see and feel happening to your fingers?

2 Sometimes we want to keep things cold. Why? What temperature should your refrigerator run at? What temperature should a freezer run at? Why are these temperatures different?

3 Do some people feel the cold more than others? Design an investigation to find out.

14·6 *Life on the edge*

Babies at risk

Ninety-three out of every 100 babies born in Britain are fully developed. Very few (seven out of every 100) are born early. These are called premature babies. They are often low in weight when they are born. Most premature babies grow up to be healthy adults.

1 What does the graph show about the survival of babies with low birth weights?

2 Write down two reasons why this is happening.

3 What do you think the chart for 1989–90 would show?

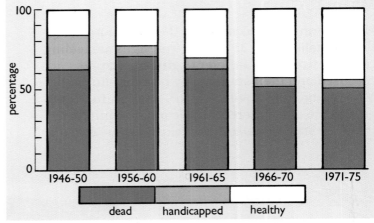

Survival rates of babies with low birth weights

Incubators

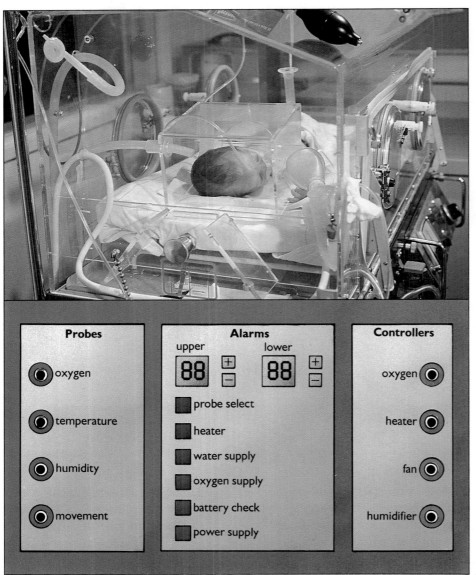

Premature babies are often cared for in machines called incubators. This protects the baby for its first few weeks growth. It controls the baby's environment until the baby has developed enough to cope with the harsher world outside.

● Look at the photograph of an incubator on the left. Make a list of the important parts of an incubator. Next to each part write down why it is needed.

Control panel

The drawing shows the control panel of a modern incubator. The blue points are for probes which measure things about the conditions in the incubator. The red points are for control lines which can change the things going into the incubator. These probes and controllers are monitored and organised by a computer program. This must be given information about the child by the nurses and doctors caring for it.

◀ *Incubator control panel*

Keeping watch

The programmers will work out a flow chart, like the one shown, to control the incubator.

4 Why is the oxygen level kept so high? The normal level in the air is only 21%.

5 How dangerous would it be if the oxygen probe:
- kept over-estimating the level of oxygen in the incubator?
- kept under-estimating the level of oxygen in the incubator?

● Use the oxygen control flow chart shown as a model. Write out a chart for keeping the baby at the right temperature. Look at the probes and controllers shown on the panel to help you.

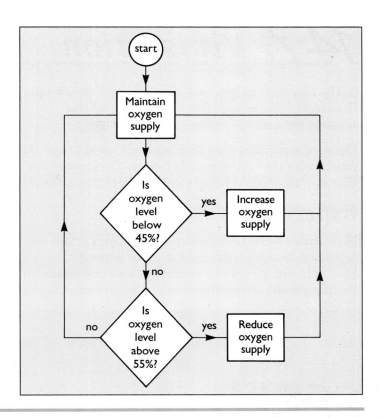

Living longer

We live much longer now than we did 200 years ago.

	Babies born per 100 000 people	Babies who die within 5 days of birth per 100 000 babies born	Mothers who die giving birth per 100 000 babies born	Deaths caused by measles per 100 000 sufferers	Average age at death (years)
1800	40	162	502	530	37
1850	35	147	481	400	41
1900	27	151	467	330	50
1950	18	18	78	4	67

6 What other changes are shown in the table here?

7 Write down as many reasons as possible to explain the changes you can see.

8 What do you think the figures for AD 2000 will be? Will they be better or worse than the ones for 1980? Write down your predictions for AD 2000. Explain how you worked out your answers.

EXTRAS

1 Write a BASIC program to control the temperature of an incubator.

2 You have been involved in a plane crash. Most of the passengers have survived. You are many kilometres from any help although the captain expects rescuers to arrive within 72 hours. The shock has caused a woman to deliver a premature baby. The little boy weighs only 2 kilograms. What can you do to keep him alive until help arrives?

3 The incubator measures and controls the baby's environment. A different machine is needed to measure things about the baby itself. This machine can often measure the baby's heart rate, blood pressure and temperature. Doctors are also interested in the baby's movements. Design a machine which will detect whenever a baby moves.

14·7 Vivisection

In the last section you saw how we are living longer than ever before. You also thought about the reasons for this.

Doctors would say that new and powerful drugs are one reason that our health is better. These can cure diseases that killed people only twenty years ago.

Experiments on animals

New drugs need to be tested. Sometimes drugs are tested on live animals. This is done in medical research and for testing cosmetics and dog foods. People almost always have strong views about it.

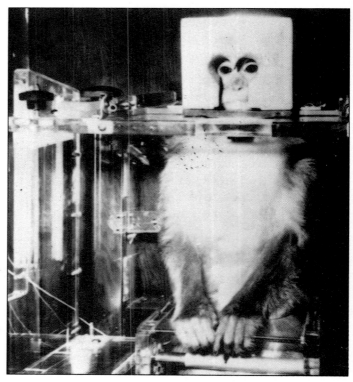

This monkey is about to have a laser beam shone into its eyes to test its reactions

Chimpanzees bred for research

Dave

'People tell me vivisection is okay in medical research. They say that, to be sure new drugs are safe, they must be tested on animals.

But the drug Opren killed 100 people when it was released in 1981. Another drug, Eraldin, made some patients blind. Thalidomide caused terrible deformities in babies. All of these drugs were said to be safe after animal testing. So vivisection does not always work.

In some cases, the same tests are being done over and over again in different laboratories. But still the results are unreliable.

Other ways of doing research already exist. We can grow human cells in test tubes to try out drugs. Chemical analysis and computer models can be used. Many of our most useful drugs like aspirin and quinine were developed from traditional medicines. These had never been tested on animals.

Most of the great killers in the world are to do with bad diet, smoking, poverty and pollution. These cannot be cured by drugs. We should stop pretending that drugs can cure us. Animals do not need to continue to suffer. We can already prevent so many diseases — why don't we do it?'

Nicola

'Vivisection always produces an emotional response. Almost everything written about it seems to be biased. This does not help people to make up their minds.

We seem to believe that scientists enjoy making animals suffer in pointless experiments. In fact, people researching new drugs are doing this to help humanity. Scientists developing safe, effective drugs are very caring or they wouldn't be bothering to do that kind of work! Many companies also have a vet to look after their animals. Many are treated better than some of the pets abandoned after Christmas.

All of the tests are not horrific torture sessions! Any experiment which caused too much suffering would be useless because the animal would not react in a normal way. Even the ones done without painkillers often only involve a single injection or dose of a drug.

To say vivisection is to blame for Thalidomide or Opren disasters is unfair. Vivisection might not always work but it has shown up some problems. It has kept some dangerous drugs off the market. If something else was as good why aren't scientists using it?'

Communicating

Who do you agree with?

- Make a list of all the facts Dave uses in his argument. Facts are the things that are **true**.
- Then make a list of all the opinions he uses. These are what he **believes**.
- Now do the same for Nicola's view.
- Who do you agree with? Discuss your ideas with your friends. It might be useful for you to note down some ideas as you talk.

- Prepare a script for a fifteen second television advertisement. It should put forward your own viewpoint. The script must contain
  – the text of the commentary you will use,
  – descriptions or drawings of the pictures you want to use,
  – any suitable soundtrack,
- If you get the chance, make a video recording of your advertisement.

EXTRAS

1 Medical research is only one aspect of animal experiments.
(a) What do you feel about using animals for testing cosmetics or washing-up liquids? What about furs? Leather shoes? Eating meat?
(b) Design a survey to find out what people think about one of these issues. Try it out on your family and friends.

2 (a) What medicines have you used during the last year? Design and carry out a survey to find out what medicines have been used by members of your class over the last year.
(b) What differences would you expect if you did the same survey among a group of old age pensioners?

3 What do cold cures contain? Make a list of the active ingredients (these are listed on the packet) for each brand.
  – Can you see any difference between them all?
  – Which brand do people prefer?
  – Why do people prefer these?

14·8 Look-alikes?

Photofit pictures are often used by police when they are looking for people 'to help them with their enquiries'. But how good are they?

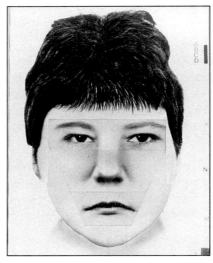

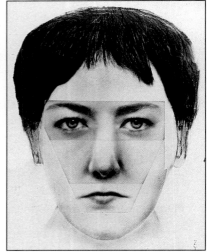

1 Are these pictures of the same person? Or three different people?

Observing

- Try to develop a system for describing people in your group. Perhaps you could: give people codes based on their height? or eye colour? or hair colour?

2 How many bits of code do you need to provide a foolproof system for your whole class?
- Use your findings to design an identity card.

Disguises

- How easy is it to recognise someone who is in disguise? Try to disguise photographs of well known people.

3 Who is most difficult to disguise?

4 What parts of the picture are important clues?

- Cartoons often look very different from the people they are supposed to show. Use your coding system to describe someone using a real photograph. Then use the same system to code a cartoon.

5 Do they produce the same result?

6 What clues do the cartoons have that are missing from the photographs?

EXTRAS

1 Can you tell who people are from pictures of them when they were younger?

2 Draw a cartoon of a famous person (or yourself). What clues will you use to make it clear who you are drawing?

3 Advertisers use images of people to sell their products. Collect some advertisements and think about why the people in them were chosen.
(**a**) Make a list of advertisements and write down a note to say what the people in them look like.

(**b**) Which types of advertisements are the most unrealistic?
(**c**) If the advertisements are full of people who are not 'normal', why do they work? What messages are they trying to get across?

14·9 Passing the message on

You will find the reference section on the following pages useful to answer the questions on this page.

1
Pick a simple job. It could be making a cup of tea or wiring a plug or cleaning your teeth. Prepare a set of instructions for someone who does not know how to do the job. How would you pass on your instructions to:
– someone who can speak English but cannot read?
– someone who cannot speak or read English?
– someone who cannot see or hear?
● What special ways do you use to get your message across?
● Which method of passing on information is least likely to cause confusion?
● Which method is most difficult to use?

Speaking louder doesn't help!

2
Some of the words on pages 45 to 49 are in bold type. Make a list of these words. Next to each one write down what it means.

3
One of the most common ways of storing information is in a book. Sometimes this information can be very hard to use. Prepare a section for a book on genes. It must be easy for 13-year-old students to understand.

GENES FOR TEENS

5
Prepare a leaflet for a doctor's waiting room. It should explain what decides whether a baby will be male or female.

6
A company has produced a new drug called the Y-booster. It is supposed to increase the production of Y-chromosome sperms and slow down the production of X-chromosome sperms.
● What effect will this have on the number of male and female babies born?
● Can you think of any situations where the drug would have advantages?
● Can you think of any situations where the drug would have disadvantages?

7
Science fiction stories often have machines for growing babies outside the mother. Sperm and eggs are mixed in a sort of glass tube and the baby grows from there.
● Draw a design for one of these machines. Your design must show how the growing baby is cared for and protected.
● What are the advantages of this technology? How could it help human beings?
● What are the dangers of this technology? How could it harm human beings?

8
Paul looked perfectly healthy when he was born. His parents were told he had cystic fibrosis when he was 6 months old. How did they feel?
● Write a script of the first time they sit down together to talk about it.
Paul wants to go to university to study medicine.
● Write a script for the day Paul gets his examination results. He is talking to his mum just after the letter arrived. She tells him about her worries for him for the first time.
● If you can, record the scenes on a tape as a radio play.

Planning

Twins
4 If you are one of twins, does that mean your children are likely to be twins? What sort of information do you need to investigate this? Where can you find this information and how would you interpret it?

Look at the pictures below. The objects are all designed
to code information about something.

14 REFERENCE 2: *Genes*

Making babies

Human beings pass coded information from parent to child. Instructions for the growing child to build blood cells, bone and brain are needed. How is this information coded?

In the last century some scientists thought the **sperm** contained a small model of an adult. This was planted inside the mother. It grew there for nine months until it was born. The woman had no control over what the growing child would look like. Others thought only the mother contained the seed. The smell of the sperm made the seed develop into the new child.

We now know that mother and father are equally important. Each passes on a set of instructions to the new **organism**. But how are these instructions coded? What would they be like?

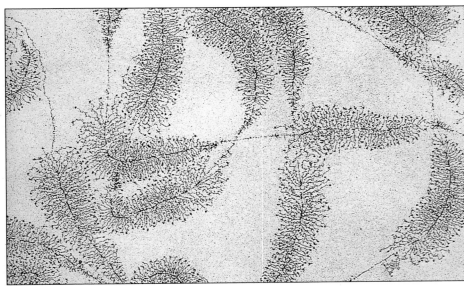

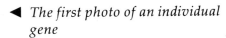

◀ *The first photo of an individual gene*

Genes

Scientists use some of the most modern techniques to look for these instructions. The name **gene** is used to describe one particular instruction. A gene is a length of a special chemical called **DNA** which is found in the **nucleus** of all human **cells**.

Chromosomes

Each gene is connected to other genes by more DNA. A package of genes is called a **chromosome**. The chromosomes below are taken from a human being. They contain thousands of genes stuck together in a string.

The chromosomes are normally stored in the nucleus of the cell. Human beings have 46 chromosomes organised into 23 pairs.

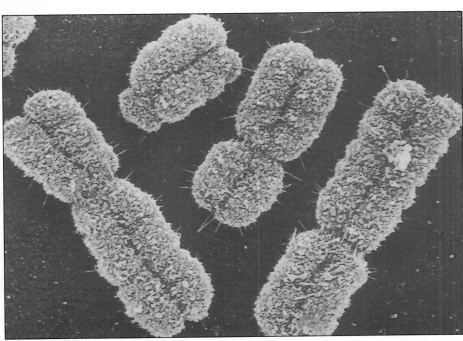

◀ *Human chromosomes*

1 Cell before division

2 Chromosomes arrange themselves in pairs along middle of cell.

3 Chromosomes are copied to give two pairs.

Making sperms and eggs

Sperm and **egg cells** are different from other body cells. They have been made by a special kind of cell division. When eggs and sperms are made the number of chromosomes in a cell is halved.

The diagram shows what would happen with a cell that had only six chromosomes. Some insects have this number. In humans the diagram would be much more complicated but would follow the same pattern.

1 How many chromosomes does human sperm have?
2 How many chromosomes does a human egg have?

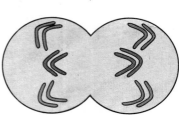

4 Cell splits, one pair of chromosomes going into each new cell.

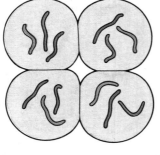

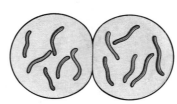

5 Cells divide again, one chromosome going into each new cell.

A special kind of cell division

Look at the photograph of a magnified human sperm.
3 Which is the most important part?
4 Why do you think this?

Look at the picture of a magnified human egg. It is much bigger than the sperm.
5 Why do you think this is?
6 Why does the egg have no tail?

The new organism begins as a tiny speck formed by the joining of one sperm with one egg. The new cell, called a **zygote**, then starts to divide and grow. It uses information from the sperm and egg chromosomes. These tell it how to build all the structures needed for independent life.
7 How many chromosomes will the **fertilised** egg have?

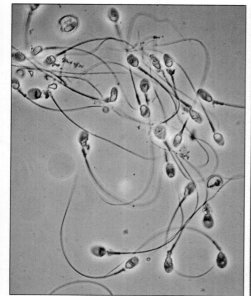

Human sperms: each is about 0.03 mm long

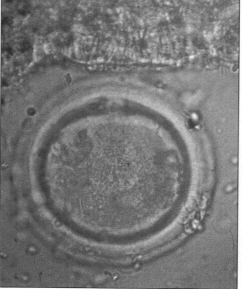

Human egg, about 0.15 mm across

'Everyone makes jokes about it, of course, but I never thought that I would really have twins. I suppose I did feel a bit big compared with the time I was carrying Tom. I thought this was because it was the second child. The first time I had a scan the doctor asked me about twins in my family. I think I guessed it would be twins then. All I can remember thinking is that we'd have to get another cot!'

'When Sarah told me I kept asking stupid questions like "Are you sure?" and "Do you think they've made a mistake?". It took a few minutes to really settle in! I suppose I was a bit concerned at first. How would we cope with two extras instead of one? How would the birth be for Sarah?
In the end it was all OK. The birth was not too bad and Tom ended up with two beautiful baby sisters. We wouldn't change them for the world now!'

How are twins formed?

Mark and Sarah's twins were one of the roughly 8000 pairs born in Britain every year. Nearly 2000 of these are **identical twins**.

These are formed when one sperm and one egg join to make one zygote. Normally this egg will divide to produce one baby. Sometimes this zygote divides into two cells and each of these two cells grows into a complete baby. Identical twins produced like this have the same genes, share one **placenta** and are always the same sex. Doctors do not know why this happens.

The remaining 6000 twins are known as **fraternal** or **non-identical twins**. These are formed when two eggs are released from the ovaries at the same time. These eggs are both fertilised by sperms and develop into separate babies each with its own placenta. They are as similar as brothers or sisters of the same age. They came from different eggs and sperms and can be different sexes.

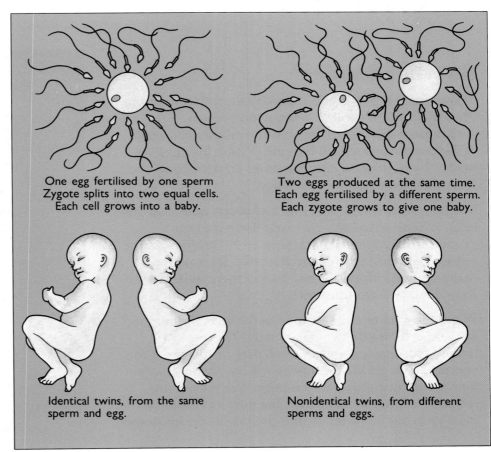

One egg fertilised by one sperm Zygote splits into two equal cells. Each cell grows into a baby.

Two eggs produced at the same time. Each egg fertilised by a different sperm. Each zygote grows to give one baby.

Identical twins, from the same sperm and egg.

Nonidentical twins, from different sperms and eggs.

REFERENCE 5: Boy or girl?

There are roughly the same number of men alive in the world as women. Roughly the same numbers are born.

Sometimes the pattern seems to break down, though. The Felton family are mum, dad and eleven boys. Why no girls?

Even more surprising is the family of boys studied by a scientist called Fred Harris. He showed a family tree going back for ten generations. In all that time only two girls were born and 33 sons.

An all-girl family

The Felton family is far from average. Their 'cricket team' of boys is helping scientists studying inherited illnesses

So what decides?

The sex of children is controlled by the father's sperm. The egg from the mother always contains an **X-chromosome**. This is because the mother has a pair of X-chromosomes in all her cells. When the eggs are made, the number of chromosomes is halved and one X-chromosome gets into each egg.

The father has one X- and one **Y-chromosome** in all his cells. When the sperms are made there are two possibilities: a sperm containing an X-chromosome or a sperm containing a Y-chromosome. The male will make millions of sperms and half of them will carry an X- and half a Y-chromosome.

When the man and the woman make love, the sperms are released into the woman's body. They swim towards the **egg** and one of them may fertilise it. If the **sperm** carries an X-chromosome, then a female (with two X-chromosomes) will be formed. If the sperm carries a Y-chromosome, then the new baby will be male with one X-chromosome and one Y-chromosome.

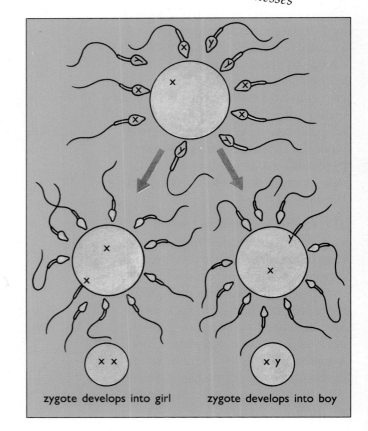

zygote develops into girl   zygote develops into boy

REFERENCE 6: *Inherited illnesses*

Margaret and Geoffrey have a little boy called Steven. He is ten years old and suffers from cystic fibrosis. This means that some of the glands in his body do not work well. His lungs and digestive system are particularly affected. If he does not receive treatment, he will suffer from lung infections and be unable to digest his food properly.

Cystic fibrosis is caused by a faulty gene. For a child to have cystic fibrosis, both parents must pass on this faulty gene. In 1989, scientists identified the faulty gene but the disease cannot yet be cured.

The faulty gene is a small section of chromosome. It should give the cell information to build a special protein. This protein helps to control things passing in and out of the body's cells. Steven notices two effects of the faulty gene:
– his lungs tend to fill up with sticky mucus,
– his gut cannot make the enzymes needed to digest food properly.

Steven lives a fairly normal life

Doctors can help Steven. Regular deep breathing exercises and physiotherapy help to drain his lungs. Special enzymes can be sprinkled on his food to help his digestion. He will be able to lead a fairly normal life though he will always need to be careful about lung infections. The symptoms of cystic fibrosis are not always the same strength. Some patients hardly know they have the disease and others are seriously ill.

Margaret and Geoffrey both have the damaged gene. They are called **carriers**. They each have a spare good gene as well so they are not affected. Mothers can be tested quite early in pregnancy (at 6-10 weeks and at 18 weeks), to see if their baby is at risk. It is also possible to detect some carriers of the damaged gene in families that are at risk. Otherwise, the parents may not know about the problem until after the baby is born.

If Geoffrey and Margaret have another baby, there is a one in four chance that it will also have cystic fibrosis. There is a one in four chance that every baby they have will suffer from cystic fibrosis.

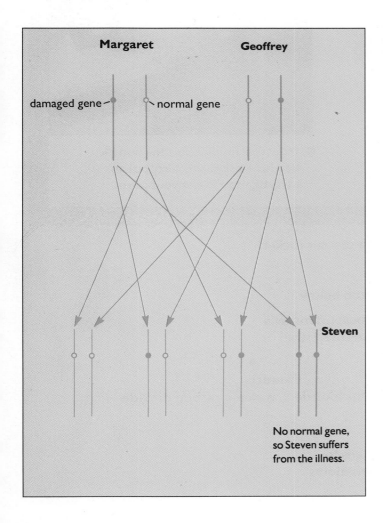

Margaret — Geoffrey

damaged gene — normal gene

Steven

No normal gene, so Steven suffers from the illness.

15 REACTIONS
15.1 A rocket reaction

Chemical reactions make new substances. Signs of a chemical reaction are:
- the new substance looks different from the starting mixture
- it is hard to change the new substance back into the starting mixture
- the mixture gets hotter or colder during the reaction

Reactions can be very powerful; enough to propel a rocket.

● What else might affect the bung's height? Design and carry out an investigation to test your ideas.

Investigating

Rocket chemistry

- In a test tube, mix sodium hydrogencarbonate ('bicarb') powder and some dilute hydrochloric acid. What happens?
- Now try the same in a plastic bottle with a rubber bung. First put a little powder in the bottle. Then add a little acid and put the bung in quickly (but not too tightly).
- What affects how high the bung goes? Design investigations to answer some of the questions below.

1 Which dilute acid gives the best result?
2 Does chilled acid work as well as acid at room temperature
3 How does the concentration of the acid affect the height the bung reaches?
4 What is the best mix of acid and 'bicarb'?

When your teacher has checked your plan, carry it out.

5 How do you know there is a chemical reaction going on in your rocket?
6 How do you make the bung go further?
7 What safety precautions do you take? Why?
8 What makes the bung take off? (Hint: look at the equation below.)

You can use an equation to describe what happens in the rocket. This tells you the chemicals used (the *reactants*) and the chemicals produced (the *products*). For the rocket, the equation is:

Reactants   **Products**

hydrochloric acid + sodium hydrogencarbonate → sodium chloride + water + carbon dioxide

To react or not?

Only some chemicals react when mixed. For chemical changes to happen, the substances need to be reactive enough and their atoms and molecules need to get close to each other.

Slow and fast reactions

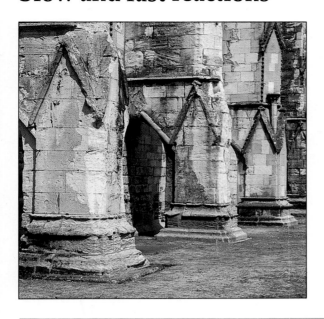

Sand and water do not react because sand is not reactive enough.

Limestone and acid rain react slowly. Acid rain is a very dilute acid. It can only reach the outside of the limestone block.

Hydrochloric acid and sodium hydrogencarbonate powder react quickly. This acid is more concentrated than acid rain. It can also attack a lot of powder at once because powder has much more surface than a lump.

◀ *This limestone has been reacting with rain for centuries*

Gunpowder

Explosives use a fine powder of very reactive particles that are well mixed. A gunpowder explosion shows how fast chemicals can react. It was probably invented in China. In AD 850 the chemist Cheng Yin wrote in a book:

'Some have heated together sulphur, realgar, and saltpetre with honey; smoke and flames result, so that their hands and faces have been burned, and even the whole house where they were working burned down.'

This seems to be the first time anyone wrote about an exploding mixture. Unfortunately, other people ignored the warning, and many blew themselves up.

By AD 1000, Chinese chemists had got the mixture just right. In AD 1044, the writer Tseng Kung-Liang published details of the formula in a book. Gunpowder was often used in rockets, grenades and flame-throwers in battles.

Arab chemists got the formula in about AD 1250. By about AD 1300, gunpowder weapons arrived in Europe. Nowadays, gunpowder is used mainly in fireworks.

A 13th century Chinese picture of a bursting bomb-shell

⚠ Never experiment with fireworks or gunpowder.

EXTRAS

1 Make two lists: one of fast and one of slow reactions you see every day. (Hint: rusting is a slow reaction.)

2 A toy company is making a rocket kit for nine-year-old children. It uses acid and 'bicarb' like your rocket. The manufacturers want the kit to look scientific, so that people will buy it. They need a good explanation for nine-year-olds of how it works. Design a leaflet that they can include in their kits. Include a safety warning. Diagrams might help!

15·2 Kitchen chemistry

A kitchen is full of chemical reactions.

● List the ones you can find in the drawing.

1 How do you know they are reactions?
2 Can you think of others that happen in your kitchen?

Making substances react ⚠️ 🥽

Reactive substances will react with many other substances. Unreactive substances may need heating or shaking to help them to react. Some substances do not react at all.

● Find out what these substances need to react:
  – copper(II)sulphate crystals,
  – magnesium ribbon,
  – washing soda,
  – iron filings,
  – eggshell.

● You can try:
  – heating a small amount on a metal tray,
  – mixing it with water (Watch to see if the chemical dissolves or reacts. If it dissolves, you can get it back easily.),
  – mixing it with a dilute alkali,
  – mixing it with a dilute acid.

● Think safe when doing these investigations.
  – Always wear goggles.
  – If you get any substance on you, wash it off with water and tell your teacher.

● After each investigation write a report, saying:
  – if there is a chemical reaction,
  – how you know there is a reaction.

Why does gas burn?

One important kitchen reaction is burning gas. To understand it you have to understand atoms. Atoms are the tiny particles that substances are made from. About one hundred million hydrogen atoms end to end measure one centimetre.

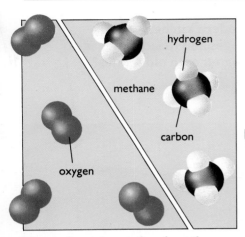

Natural gas is made of methane molecules. Each molecule contains one carbon atom joined to four hydrogen atoms. Oxygen gas contains oxygen atoms joined in pairs.

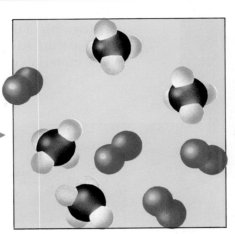

Oxygen and methane molecules are moving all the time. They bump into each other. At room temperature, they do not hit each other hard enough to do anything except bounce off.

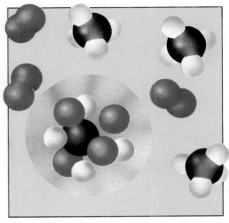

A flame in the mixture makes the molecules go faster. The atoms in each molecule also start to vibrate more. Now the molecules crash into each other harder. The extra energy breaks the molecules and rearranges the atoms.

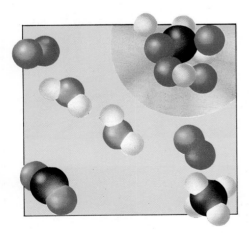

◀ The products of the reaction are water and carbon dioxide. Heat is also produced which is useful for cooking. The heat makes other gas molecules move faster, so they can also react.

The equation for the gas reaction is:

methane + oxygen → water (hydrogen oxide) + carbon dioxide

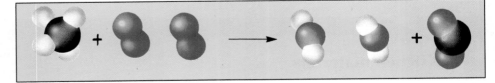

EXTRAS

1 Investigate which acids at home are most ⚠ reactive. You could test vinegar, Coke, fruit juices, etc.

Test their reaction with washing soda, stomach powder or baking powder. How will you decide which acid is most reactive?

2 Do a plan for an investigation to answer one of these questions:
(a) What effect does the strength of the acid have on the reaction with limestone?
(b) What effect does the size of the limestone pieces have?
(c) Predict what you think will happen if you try the investigation.

15·3 Choosing materials

Kitchen worktops used to be made of wood. Wood is hard-wearing, fairly easy to clean and it used to be quite cheap. Modern work surfaces are mostly made of plastic laminate. Plastic is hard-wearing and easily cleaned. It also comes in bright colours and is simple to mass-produce. Both wood and plastic make good materials for worktops.

1 What other new materials can you see in the photograph of the modern kitchen?
2 What are the advantages and disadvantages of these materials compared with older ones?

▲ *A kitchen of a hundred years ago in Broderick Castle*

A modern kitchen ▶

Observing

Kitchen materials
Choose at least five things from your kitchen at home. Describe each of them.

3 What does it look like?
4 What is it used for?
5 What is it made of?
6 Why is it made of that material?

Testing materials

● Find materials which would be good as:

   – a container for Coke,   – an oven-proof dish,   – a filling for a tooth,   – a waterproof wrap for frozen peas.

  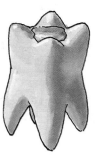 

● Plan some tests. You will need to do:
   – physical tests (Is it strong? Is it easy to shape? Does it shatter?),
   – chemical tests (Does it rot? Is it reactive?).
Remember to *think safe*. You must not taste any of the materials!

Check your plan with your teacher before starting any investigations.

Testing metals

● Plan an investigation to find out how reactive metals are.
Your aim is to finish up with a list of metals with the most reactive at the top. Your teacher must see your plan before you carry it out. She or he may also show you tests that are too dangerous for you to do.
● When you have done or seen the tests, make a display of your group's results.
● Look at other groups' results. Are your lists the same?

What to look for

Test	Very reactive metal	Reactive metal	Unreactive metal
Reaction in air	reacts without heating	reacts when heated	no change (but may melt)
Reaction in water	reacts with cold water	reacts with hot water	no reaction
Reaction in dilute acid	violent reaction (dangerous)	reacts quickly	reacts slowly or not at all

EXTRAS

1 Choose two metals in your home that you have not tested in class. For example, chromium plating on a bicycle, steel (nails), brass (door handle, ornament). Say where you would put them in your reactivity list. Explain your answer.

2 Copper is less reactive than lead.
(a) Why does this make copper better for water pipes in your home?
(b) Why do some homes now have plastic water pipes?

Planning

3 One way of getting rid of nuclear waste is to bury it.
(a) What material would you use to make a container for this waste? (See Section 13.11.)
(b) Plan an investigation to find out which affects the strength of the container more:
– the type of material used,
– the thickness of the material.

You have used many chemicals in your science lessons. You use others, like water and sugar, without even thinking about them.

Most chemicals are very complicated. They are made from different atoms joined in different ways. Fortunately there are not many types of atom.

Some chemicals contain only one type of atom. These chemicals are elements. All the atoms in an element are the same.

Different elements react together to make compounds. Most of the things around us are compounds. These compounds are usually made of some of the elements listed here.

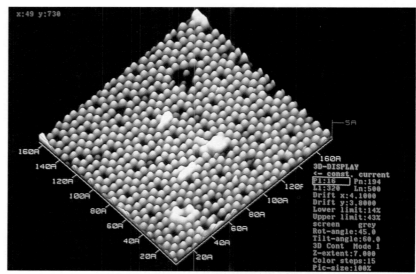

Silicon atoms photographed with a tunnelling electron microscope

Observing

Sorting elements into groups

● Use the information and your own tests to sort elements into three or four groups. Try to choose your groups so that the elements in each group behave in the same way. Your teacher may be able to show you some other elements. Here are some things to look for:

– Is the element reactive or not reactive?
– Does it look shiny or dull?
– Is it hard or soft?
– Does it bend or does it snap?
– Can it conduct electricity or not?
You may think of some other tests as well

● Use your results to make a key to identify the elements you have seen.

1 Which of your element groups would you put these elements in? Explain your choices.

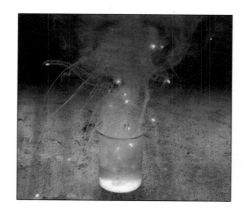

Iodine forms brittle purple-black crystals. The crystals become a purple gas when they are heated gently. Iodine does not react with oxygen nor conduct electricity.

Rubidium is very rare. It is a soft grey metal. It reacts so easily with the air that it has to be kept in oil. It explodes when it is dropped into cold water.

Only 0.05% of the atmosphere is helium. Helium is lighter than air and has no colour or smell. It does not react easily with other chemicals.

Aluminium Al Solid
Occurrence 8.5%
Relative atomic mass 27
Aluminium is a light, strong metal. It is found in nature as bauxite. We can extract the metal by melting it and passing an electric current through the molten ore. A temperature of 900°C is needed. Rubies and sapphires are coloured crystals of aluminium oxide. Aluminium is used for drinks cans and cooking foil. Aluminium alloys are used in aircraft.

Argon Ar Gas
Occurrence 0.000004%
Relative atomic mass 40
Argon is an inert, colourless gas. It will not react easily with anything. It can be extracted from the air. It is sometimes used to fill light bulbs because it does not react with the hot filament. Argon is more commonly used in fluorescent tubes.

A light bulb filled with argon

Barium Ba Solid
Occurrence 0.1%
Relative atomic mass 137
Barium is a hard metal. It is useful because X-rays cannot pass through its compounds. People with digestive problems are sometimes given a 'meal' containing barium compounds. An X-ray of the patient shows the gut in white.

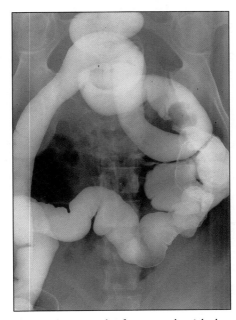

X-ray photograph of a stomach with the intestines highlighted by barium meal

Beryllium Be Solid
Occurrence 0.01%
Relative atomic mass 9
A very light, strong element that conducts heat well but cannot conduct electricity. Radiation can pass straight through beryllium and it has many very specialised uses in the aerospace industry and X-ray measuring machines. Beryllium oxide is used in some electronic components.

Boron B Solid
Occurrence 0.0003%
Relative atomic mass 11
Boron is usually seen as a black powder. It is very hard and unreactive. Compounds of boron can be used to make a kind of glass. Borax is a compound of boron used in some fireproofing chemicals.

Bromine Br Liquid
Occurrence 0.00004%
Relative atomic mass 80
Bromine is a heavy, reddish-coloured liquid. It is poisonous and can bleach

indicator paper white. It is extracted from sea water. Bromine compounds are used in Jacuzzis to keep them free of germs in the same way as chlorine is used in swimming pools.

Calcium Ca Solid
Occurrence 3.8%
Relative atomic mass 40
Calcium is a grey, brittle metal. It reacts slowly with water to produce hydrogen and a milky white alkali, calcium hydroxide. Calcium is found in compounds all round us: limestone, lime, bones, teeth and the shells of sea creatures. Milk and cheese are good sources of calcium in food.

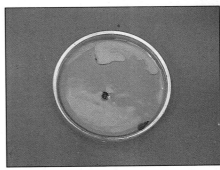

Calcium metal in water

Carbon C Solid
Occurrence 0.03%
Relative atomic mass 12
Carbon is a black solid that has many forms, from soft graphite (pencil 'lead') to diamond. Carbon is the base of many giant molecules. Many are part of every living thing. Fossil fuels contain carbon. The carbon dioxide that is made when these fuels burn may be causing the Earth to warm up.

Chlorine Cl Gas
Occurrence 0.03%
Relative atomic mass 35
Chlorine is a poisonous, greenish-yellow gas. It is used to clean tap water and keep swimming pools free of germs. Chlorine has many other uses, including the manufacture of plastics, dyes and drugs.

Copper Cu Solid
Occurrence 0.003%
Relative atomic mass 64
Copper is a soft, orange-coloured metal that conducts heat and electricity very well. It is used in electrical wires and water pipes in homes. It is not very reactive and is often mixed with other metals to make useful alloys. Brass is a mixture of 30% copper and 70% zinc.

Copper tubing

Fluorine F Gas
Occurrence 0.1%
Relative atomic mass 19
Fluorine is a very reactive gas. With hydrogen it produces an acid gas which can dissolve glass. CFCs are fluorine compounds which are thought to damage the ozone layer. CFCs are used to make expanded plastic cups and in refrigerators and aerosol sprays. PTFE is a useful plastic that contains fluorine.

Gold Au Solid
Occurrence 0.000 000 5%
Relative atomic mass 197
Gold is a soft, yellow metal that is found in nature as an unreacted element. For this reason, it was one of the first metals used by human beings. It is not attacked by acids and lasts thousands of years without tarnishing. It is used in delicate electronic components and jewellery.

Making gold jewellery in Ghana

Hydrogen H Gas
Occurrence 0.1%
Relative atomic mass 1
Hydrogen is the most common element in the universe and is also the lightest. It has no taste, smell or colour and burns very rapidly in oxygen to produce water. Hydrogen is found in many other compounds. e.g. acids, carbohydrates like sugar, proteins, fats and wood. The airship *Hindenburg* was filled with hydrogen. A spark ignited it and the whole ship burned as the gas reacted with air.

Destruction of the Hindenburg *near New York in 1937*

Iron Fe Solid
Occurrence 5.2%
Relative atomic mass 56
Iron is the most commonly used metal in the world. Pure iron rusts in damp air, so it is usually made into alloys or plated with other metals. Steels are alloys of iron with small amounts of other metals and carbon.

Working in a Sheffield iron foundry

Krypton Kr Gas
Occurrence 0.000 000 02%
Relative atomic mass 84
Krypton is an inert gas that does not react easily with anything. It can be extracted from the air. It does not smell and has no colour or taste. It is used to fill light bulbs and fluorescent tubes.

Lead Pb Solid
Occurrence 0.002%
Relative atomic mass 207
Lead is a soft, heavy, grey metal found mainly as the mineral galena. There are often small amounts of gold and silver mixed in with the ore. Lead has been used for many years on roofs and water pipes because it is easy to shape and reacts only very slowly with water. Pewter tankards are made from an alloy of 20% lead and 80% tin.

Lithium Li Solid
Occurrence 0.01%
Relative atomic mass 7
Lithium is a soft, light metal. It reacts quickly with cold water, making hydrogen gas and an alkaline solution. It reacts slowly with the air and is usually stored under oil.

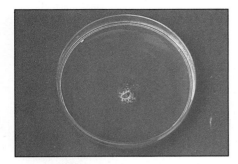

Lithium metal in water

Magnesium Mg Solid
Occurrence 2.2%
Relative atomic mass 24
Magnesium is a light metal that burns easily with a bright white light in oxygen. It reacts with water to give off hydrogen and leave an alkaline solution. Early photographers used magnesium powder as a flash. Nowadays, magnesium is used in lightweight alloys.

A magnesium-based firework

Manganese Mn Solid
Occurrence 0.1%
Relative atomic mass 55
Manganese is a grey metal. It is used to make very hard alloys of steel with iron. Lumps of manganese, called nodules, have been found lying on the sea bed in parts of the deep ocean. In the future, they may be collected for use.

Mercury Hg Liquid
Occurrence 0.00005%
Relative atomic mass 201
Mercury is the only metal which is liquid at room temperatures. It freezes at −39°C. Mercury compounds are often very poisonous. However, an amalgam (a kind of alloy) can be made which is used for fillings for teeth. The most important mercury ore is cinnabar, mercury sulphide.

Metallic mercury at room temperature

Neon Ne Gas
Occurrence 0.000 000 007%
Relative atomic mass 20
Neon is an inert gas and does not react easily with anything. It has no taste, smell or colour. When a high voltage is connected to a tube of neon gas, the neon atoms absorb some of the energy. The atoms give the energy out again as bright red light. Advertising signs often use neon tubes for red light.

Nitrogen N Gas
Occurrence 0.02%
Relative atomic mass 14
Nitrogen is a colourless gas with no smell or taste. It makes up 80% of the air. Nitrogen does not react very well but is part of many important compounds. Protein in living things, nylon, fertilisers, nitric acid, gunpowder and other explosives contain nitrogen.

Oxygen O Gas
Occurrence 49.9%
Relative atomic mass 16
20% of the air is oxygen. It is a colourless, tasteless gas with no smell. It is slightly heavier than air. Oxygen is vital for human beings. Patients with weak lungs are often given extra oxygen in hospitals. Many things contain compounds of oxygen joined to other elements, e.g. most foods, all living things, most everyday objects. Ozone is a form of oxygen. High up in the atmosphere, it protects us from harmful radiation. At ground level, it can actually damage the lungs.

This transplant patient has to stay in a sterile enclosure with an oxygen-rich atmosphere

Potassium K Solid
Occurrence 2.7%
Relative atomic mass 39
Potassium is a soft, grey metal that burns easily in air with a pinkish flame. It reacts rapidly with water to give off hydrogen and leave an alkaline solution. The reaction gets so hot that the hydrogen usually burns. Potassium is part of all living things and can be found in bone ash, seaweed, sheep sweat and sugar beet.

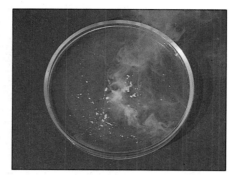

Potassium metal in water

Silicon Si Solid
Occurrence 23.8%
Relative atomic mass 28
Silicon is found as both a hard brown powder and a shiny grey crystal. It is a common element and silicon compounds are found in many rocks. Sand is silica, a compound of silicon and oxygen. Silicon can conduct electricity better than insulators but not as well as most conductors. For this reason it is called a semiconductor. It is used to make silicon chips – the basis of all calculators and computers.

Silver Ag Solid
Occurrence 0.00001%
Relative atomic mass 108
Silver is a heavy, shiny white metal often found as an impurity in lead and copper ores. Silver conducts heat and electricity better than any other element. Compounds of silver are used in photography. Silver bromide changes to silver when light falls on it. This reaction is normally slow but chemicals used in photography can speed it up to produce a picture.

Sodium Na Solid
Occurrence 3.0%
Relative atomic mass 23
Sodium is a soft, grey metal that burns easily in air. It reacts rapidly with cold water to make hydrogen gas and leave a strongly alkaline solution. The reaction gets so hot the sodium melts and floats on the surface as a shiny ball of silvery metal. Sodium compounds are found in all living things and as sodium chloride in the sea.

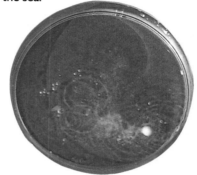

Sodium metal in water

Tin Sn Solid
Occurrence 0.004%
Relative atomic mass 119
The tin ore, cassiterite, used to be mined by the Romans in Cornwall. Tin mining has now almost stopped in Cornwall because of a fall in demand for the metal. 'Tin' cans are tin plated on to an iron alloy. Clean iron is dipped in a bath of molten tin. When it is lifted out the tin forms a thin layer covering the iron. This prevents the air from reaching the iron and making it rust.

Titanium Ti Solid
Occurrence 0.3%
Relative atomic mass 48
Titanium is a light but strong metal. It is often used with iron to make hard alloys. Titanium steel is particularly useful for parts of aircraft engines that have to stand up to very high temperatures. Titanium burns in air to produce a white oxide which is used to make white paint.

Zinc Zn Solid
Occurrence 0.06%
Relative atomic mass 65
Zinc is a hard metal which does not corrode in air. It is often used in alloys with copper. These alloys are strong and resist corrosion even in sea water. They are often used for the propellers and hulls of ocean-going ships. Zinc is sometimes used as a protective coating for other metals like iron. This is called galvanising. Some parts of cars are galvanised. The makers dip the clean iron into molten zinc.

Galvanising pipes by dipping them into a tank of molten zinc

The Periodic Table

The Periodic Table is a list of elements. You 'read' it like a book, from top left to bottom right. Along the top are elements that have light atoms. As you go across and down, the atoms in each element get heavier. Elements that come underneath each other are similar. Usually, they react the same way. Sometimes they look the same as well. The elements in one column all belong to the same *group*.

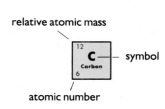

relative atomic mass — symbol — atomic number

| 12 |
| C |
| Carbon |
| 6 |

1 H Hydrogen 1																	4 He Helium 2
7 Li Lithium 3	9 Be Beryllium 4											11 B Boron 5	12 C Carbon 6	14 N Nitrogen 7	16 O Oxygen 8	19 F Fluorine 9	20 Ne Neon 10
23 Na Sodium 11	24 Mg Magnesium 12											27 Al Aluminium 13	28 Si Silicon 14	31 P Phosphorus 15	32 S Sulphur 16	35.5 Cl Chlorine 17	40 Ar Argon 18
39 K Potassium 19	40 Ca Calcium 20	45 Sc Scandium 21	48 Ti Titanium 22	51 V Vanadium 23	52 Cr Chromium 24	55 Mn Manganese 25	56 Fe Iron 26	59 Co Cobalt 27	59 Ni Nickel 28	63.5 Cu Copper 29	65 Zn Zinc 30	70 Ga Gallium 31	73 Ge Germanium 32	75 As Arsenic 33	79 Se Selenium 34	80 Br Bromine 35	84 Kr Krypton 36
85 Rb Rubidium 37	88 Sr Strontium 38	89 Y Yttrium 39	91 Zr Zirconium 40	93 Nb Niobium 41	96 Mo Molybdenum 42	Tc Technetium 43	101 Ru Ruthenium 44	103 Rh Rhodium 45	106 Pd Palladium 46	108 Ag Silver 47	112 Cd Cadmium 48	115 In Indium 49	119 Sn Tin 50	122 Sb Antimony 51	128 Te Tellurium 52	127 I Iodine 53	131 Xe Xenon 54
133 Cs Caesium 55	137 Ba Barium 56	139 La Lanthanum 57	178 Hf Hafnium 72	181 Ta Tantalum 73	184 W Tungsten 74	186 Re Rhenium 75	190 Os Osmium 76	192 Ir Iridium 77	195 Pt Platinum 78	197 Au Gold 79	201 Hg Mercury 80	204 Tl Thallium 81	207 Pb Lead 82	209 Bi Bismuth 83	Po Polonium 84	At Astatine 85	Rn Radon 86
Fr Francium 87	Ra Radium 88	Ac Actinium 89															

140 Ce Cerium 58	141 Pr Praseodymium 59	144 Nd Neodymium 60	Pm Promethium 61	150 Sm Samarium 62	152 Eu Europium 63	157 Gd Gadolinium 64	159 Tb Terbium 65	162 Dy Dysprosium 66	165 Ho Holmium 67	167 Er Erbium 68	169 Tm Thulium 69	173 Yb Ytterbium 70	175 Lu Lutetium 71
232 Th Thorium 90	Pa Protactinium 91	238 U Uranium 92	Np Neptunium 93	Pu Plutonium 94	Am Americium 95	Cm Curium 96	Bk Berkelium 97	Cf Californium 98	Es Einsteinium 99	Fm Fermium 100	Md Mendelevium 101	No Nobelium 102	Lw Lawrencium 103

- Write down the elements in one of the groups of the Periodic Table. Find out:
  - how they are alike,
  - how they are different.

- Use the group you have just investigated. Find out if the group gets more reactive, less reactive or stays the same as the elements get heavier.

- On a blank copy of the Periodic Table, use colours to show where the solids, liquids and gases are. What do you notice? Make some predictions about the elements you are not sure about.

- On another blank copy of the table, use colours to show where the metals and nonmetals are. What do you notice?

- Hydrogen is not in a group in the Periodic Table shown. Which group would you put it in? Explain how you made your choice.

EXTRAS

Communicating

1 You have to do a demonstration at a Christmas lecture for primary schools. Choose one element to talk about. Plan your lecture and demonstration to last about five minutes. Remember that eleven-year-olds will not know what an element is.

2 (a) Make a computer database of the elements you have tested. The database has to be able to tell you what the element is like and what it is used for.
(b) Are there any odd groups that do not seem to fit together? Which ones are odd? What is different about the elements in them?

15·7 Reacting gases

- The containers shown all have a gas in them. Write down a list of the gases and what they could be used for.

Making hydrogen ⚠

- Make and collect some hydrogen as shown. Take great care. Hydrogen can explode in air. Do not let any flames come near your bottle or delivery tube. You should also use a plastic flask and have a safety screen.

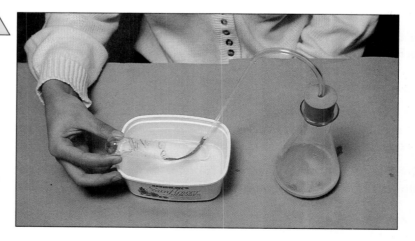

Burning hydrogen

- Test your gas well away from any hydrogen-making equipment. Watch and listen very carefully.
  - Take the bung off the test tube.
  - Quickly hold a lighted splint just above the test tube. If the tube is full of hydrogen, the gas will burn with a soft 'pop'.

- Next collect some hydrogen in a tube which is half full of air to start with.
- Light this mixture. How does it burn now? What else do you notice?
- Find out the most dangerous (noisy) mixture of air and hydrogen.

An explosive explanation

When hydrogen and oxygen react, they make water. You may see this water as condensation in the tube after you 'pop' the hydrogen.

Water is a compound. Compounds contain at least two different types of atom joined together.

1 Hydrogen and oxygen molecules mix

Both hydrogen and oxygen molecules contain two atoms. The molecules hit each other, but bounce off. They are not moving fast enough to cause any changes. No water is formed.

2 A compound, water (H_2O), is made

The heat from the lighted splint makes the molecules move faster. This makes them hit each other harder. The old molecules are broken apart and new ones are formed. Heat is given out.

3 The reaction spreads

The heat from the reaction makes the other molecules move faster. They hit each other harder. In a fraction of a second, over 1 million million million molecules in your test tube could react.

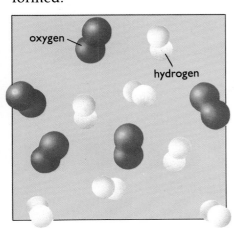

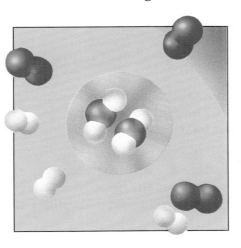

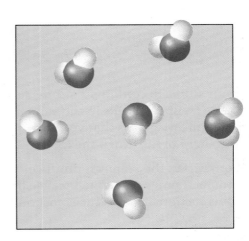

We can show this reaction in words:

hydrogen   +   oxygen   →   hydrogen oxide (water)

In symbols:

$2H_2$ + O_2 → $2H_2O$

With a diagram:

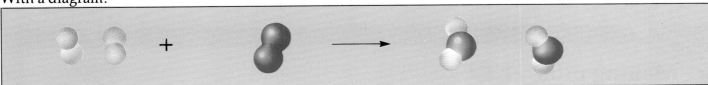

EXTRAS

1 Sulphur dioxide is a dangerous acid gas. It is made when coal burns. It dissolves in water in the air and helps to make rain acid. Design a sulphur dioxide absorber for a power station chimney. Think about:
– what you will absorb the gas with,
– how you will test that the gas has been removed.
If your design is good, you may be able to make it.

2 Draw a simple flow chart that explains exactly what happens when hydrogen 'pops' in a test tube.

3 The noisiest mixture of hydrogen and air contains about two parts of hydrogen to five parts of air. Why?

15·8 Stomach ache

Your stomach contains a strong acid compound called hydrochloric acid. It is made by special cells in the stomach wall. The acid has two jobs:
– to kill any germs that you eat with your food,
– to help break down the food.

Sometimes the stomach produces too much acid, causing stomach ache.
Stomach powders can neutralise the acid. This usually helps to reduce the pain.
The reaction also produces carbon dioxide gas. What problems might this cause?

Neutralising an acid stomach

Use 5 cm³ of dilute (1 M) hydrochloric acid in a flask as a model of an acid stomach.

Investigate which of these compounds will neutralise it. You could try:
– salt (sodium chloride),
– washing soda (sodium carbonate),
– marble (calcium carbonate chips),

– chalk (calcium carbonate powder),
– ammonia solution,
– water.

● Find out:
   – which substances work,
   – how much of each you need to neutralise the acid.

Investigating

Making pills ⚠ 😎

Medicines need to do two things. They need to start easing the pain quickly. They also need to go on working for a while.

● Use marble chips and your model stomach to find out how you can make the reaction start quickly but last for a while.
   – You cannot change the temperature of the acid. Why?

– You cannot give the patient anything that would be poisonous.
– You can make peppermint creams with a paste of icing sugar and peppermint flavouring with a little water. The sugar acts as glue. Can you use this idea to make a stomach pill?

Find a solution to the stomach pill problem. You must not swallow the pill yourself to test it!

Reaction speeds

Acid and stomach powder react when the acid particles reach the powder . Each speck of powder contains millions of calcium carbonate particles. The acid particles have to be able to hit the calcium carbonate particles hard enough to break the bonds joining the atoms.

There are three easy ways to slow the reaction down:

1 Cool the acid down
This means that the acid particles move more slowly. They do not hit the powder hard enough to react.

2 Make the acid more dilute
This means that fewer acid particles will reach the powder.

3 Make the powder into lumps
The acid can only react with the outside of the lumps at first.

Delayed-action pills

The capsule shown in the picture is one solution to the problem of supplying a steady dose of a drug. The small balls you can see contain the important drug. They are held in the capsule coat to make them easy to swallow.

Inside the body, the capsule coat dissolves quickly to release the smaller coloured balls. These dissolve at different speeds. One sort dissolves quickly to release a supply of the drug. As this is being used up in the body, the other balls are dissolving more slowly. As the first dose runs out, the next set of coloured balls break down to release their medicine.

Dissolving thread

Surgeons often need to sew together the sides of a cut to help it heal. The thread used for cuts on the body surface is a kind of cotton or synthetic thread. When the wound has healed it is cut and pulled out.

Cat gut is a kind of thread surgeons use to sew up wounds inside the body. Thread made from cat gut dissolves slowly and when the wounds has healed the thread is absorbed by the body. There are many different thicknesses and types of cat gut.

- Design an investigation to find out how long a piece of cat gut thread would take to dissolve in the body.

EXTRAS

1 (a) You have spilt some acid on your hand. Explain carefully what you would do.
(b) Why is it not a good idea to put stomach powder on the acid?

2 Wood is a mixture of compounds containing carbon and hydrogen. A bonfire is a chemical reaction between these compounds and oxygen.
(a) Do a sketch of a bonfire, showing where you would put pieces of different sizes.
(b) Explain, using the ideas on this page, how you can get wood to burn more quickly.

Some compounds are important because they help plants to grow. Most plants get these compounds from the soil. The compounds dissolve in water and pass into the plants through their roots. Compounds absorbed from the soil are usually called minerals.

▲ *Broad beans grown with nitrate fertiliser (left) and without (right)*

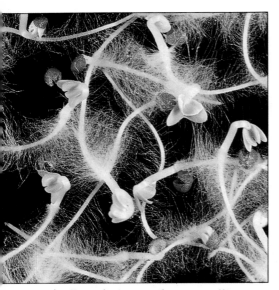

▲ *Root hairs on clover seedlings*

Manure

Fertiliser in bulk!

Element or compound?

Plants use some of the elements that minerals contain. They use nitrogen to make proteins, calcium to grow roots and potassium to grow green leaves. But these elements cannot be absorbed simply as elements.

1 What would happen if potassium metal was added to wet soil?

These elements are contained in simple compounds called mineral salts that the plant can absorb. Fertilisers contain the mineral salts that plants need. Manure is a natural fertiliser. It contains compounds of nitrogen, phosphorus, carbon, hydrogen, sulphur and potassium. These compounds break down slowly in the soil, releasing their minerals.

Artificial fertilisers are much simpler than manure. They are usually a mixture of three or four salts. A salt is made when an acid reacts with an alkali. These salts dissolve quickly in water in the soil and get into the plant.

	Carbon	Calcium	Hydrogen	Nitrogen	Oxygen	Phosphorus	Potassium	Other
ground bones	*	**	*	*	*	**	*	*
dried blood	*	*	*	**	*		*	*
farmyard manure	***	*	**	**	*	*	*	*
sewage sludge	***	*	**	**	*	*	*	*
ammonium nitrate			**	***	**			
ammonium sulphate			**	***	**			**
superphosphate		**	**		**	**		
potassium chloride							**	***
Growmore		**		**	**	**	**	

* contains the element   ** a good source of the element   *** a very good source of the element

2 Which elements seem to be important for plants to grow?

3 What else do plants need?

4 Why do some soils need fertiliser when others are fertile without any?

5 What can a farmer do to keep soil fertile without fertiliser?

6 Why is natural fertiliser better than manufactured fertiliser? (There are several reasons.)

7 Why is manufactured fertiliser used by many farmers?

Investigating

Using fertilisers

● Plan an investigation to test the ideas below. The tests will need weeks to complete; be patient. Think what you will alter, what you will measure, and when you should measure it. Get your plans checked and then try them.

– It is best to put fertiliser on a soil before you put seeds in.
– Fertilisers which contain potassium help plants stand up to frost and high temperatures.
– Fertilisers with nitrogen help leaves to grow.
– Fertilisers with phosphorus help roots to grow.

Making fertiliser

The compound ammonium sulphate is an artificial fertiliser. It is a salt made when sulphuric acid and ammonia react.

sulphuric acid + ammonia →
   ammonium sulphate

Its chemical formula is $(NH_4)_2SO_4$. Which elements make it a fertiliser? What is missing?

Basic skills

Making ammonium sulphate

You may be able to make ammonium sulphate. Keep a record of everything you see and do. Remember to think safe. Sulphuric acid is dangerous.

● At the end, do a flow drawing of your experiment. Put your results in a table.

8 How do you know that there has been a chemical reaction?

EXTRAS

1 Many people now buy 'organic vegetables'. What does the word 'organic' mean here? Why are people so keen to buy these crops, which are often much more expensive?

2 (a) Make an estimate of the cost of your fertiliser. Assume that ammonia and sulphuric acid cost 10p per 100 cm³ and heat costs 1p for 5 minutes. Estimate any other material and equipment costs.
(b) How much should you sell 100 g of fertiliser for?
(c) Are there any other costs that real fertiliser manufacturers have to include?

15·10 *Using reactions: cold packs*

Some chemical reactions produce heat and the reactants get hot. Others absorb heat and feel colder. Hot reactions like burning gas are used for cooking. Cold reactions can also be useful.

Sprained ankles and other injuries are often treated with ice packs. The cold reduces the pain and stops the joint from swelling.

Surfaces and strains

International tennis players can lose enormous amounts of money if they are injured and cannot play. The surface they play on seems to have an effect on the injury rate. The table shows the percentage of players who felt some pain when they played on different surfaces. This pain could be the beginning of a serious injury.

Gabriella Sabatini having an ankle injury treated with an ice pack

Surface	Type	Injury rate (% of players)
sand	clay	2
synthetic sand	clay	3
synthetic surfaces	hard outdoor	11
asphalt or concrete	hard outdoor	13
carpet	indoor	14
synthetic grill	indoor	17

● Draw a chart to display these figures.

1 Which types of surface have the lowest injury rate?

2 Why would this information be useful to professional tennis players?

Finding a cold reaction

You are going to make an instant cold pack from chemicals.
Discover what happens when these substances are added to water. Try to find out which has the biggest effect:
- copper(II)sulphate (white),
- ammonium chloride,
- ammonium nitrate,
- sodium chloride,
- calcium oxide.

3 How will you be sure that your test is fair?

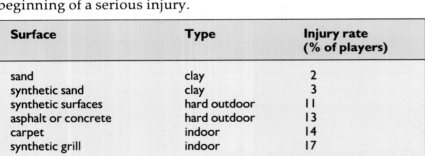

Investigating

How much to use?

● Choose a chemical which:
  - is safe,
  - gives a good temperature drop.

● Investigate how the drop in temperature depends on the amount of chemical that you use.

● Find a good way to display your results.

Designing a cold pack

The outer bag must be thick enough not to leak! The inner bag must be thin enough to burst when you squash the whole ice pack.

● Plan and carry out the investigations you will need to do to decide on the thickness of the plastic bags. Make sure you work out:
  – what you need to change,
  – what you need to keep the same,
  – how you will collect your results.

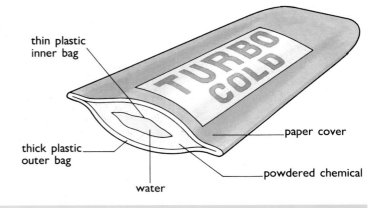

thin plastic inner bag

TURBO COLD

paper cover

thick plastic outer bag

powdered chemical

water

Communicating

Marketing the cold pack

● You will need to work out the price of your pack. What information do you need?

● How should you label your pack? Does it have to be used in a particular way? Are there any safety warnings that you should print on the pack?

● Plan an advertisement (poster or TV) to sell the ice pack.

Many a slip

What happens when you twist your ankle?

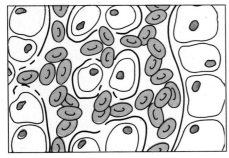

Blood vessels burst, releasing cells and plasma into tissues. The ankle swells.

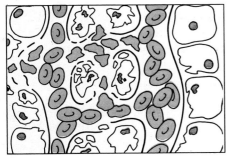

Cells die. The ankle hurts.

Coldness has two effects on the body. It reduces the sensitivity of nerves and reduces the flow of blood and other liquids.

4 How does this help with a sprained ankle?
5 Tight bandages are sometimes used for sprains. Why are these useful?
6 After about two or three days, gentle massage is useful. How does this help?

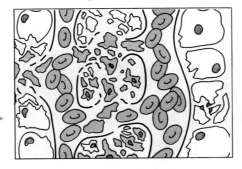

The dying cells release chemicals which bring more blood to the area. The area begins to feel hot and look pink.

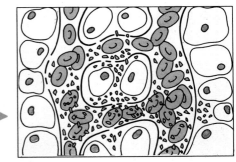

After about 24 hours, tissues begin to repair themselves. The swelling goes down as the dead cells and excess liquid drain away.

EXTRAS

1 Do a survey to find out if anyone in your class has suffered any sports injuries. Which injuries are most common? How long did they take to heal completely?

2 Can you design a heat pack? Perhaps a tin of beans that automatically warms itself when you open it? Where would this be useful?

15·11 *Using reactions: cleaning*

Many metals corrode. The metal reacts with chemicals in the air, usually oxygen or an acid. It goes dull, rusty or even green.

- Investigate a corroded metal. Find out:
  - if you can dissolve the corrosion away,
  - if you can use a chemical (acid or alkali) to remove the corrosion,
  - how mechanical methods (like scrubbing or scraping) compare with the other methods.

- If you have no corroded metal to test, you can 'corrode' some copper by heating it in a Bunsen flame for a few seconds. This makes the elements copper and oxygen react to make copper oxide:

copper + oxygen → copper oxide

- Your job is to clean it up. There are two possibilities:
  - separate the copper from the oxygen,
  - dissolve the copper oxide away to leave clean copper.

Household hints

- Present your findings as a page in a book of helpful household hints.

Coins with different amounts of corrosion

Bath stains

Bath stains can be very hard to remove. They come from hot water which contains dissolved chemicals. When the water cools, the chemicals become solid and stain the bath.

- Investigate some 'artificial' bath stain. Try to discover what will dissolve it. |W|
- Look at the chemical tests on the worksheet. You could use these to find out what chemical the stain is.

Dissolving

Some liquids can dissolve things. For example, petrol will dissolve grease.

Petrol is a *solvent*: it can dissolve grease. The grease is a *solute*: it is dissolved in the petrol. The mixture of petrol and grease is a *solution*.

When a solute dissolves, its particles spread out evenly into the solvent.
Water dissolves so many different things that it is sometimes called a 'universal solvent'.

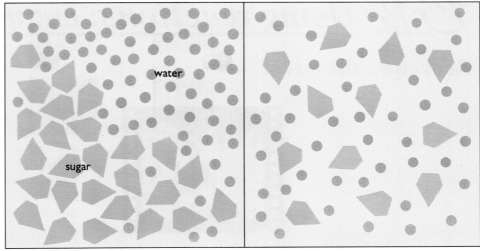

Sugar dissolving in water

Cleaning up the staff room

This sofa was found in a school staff room. Do what you can!

● Investigate how some of the stains can be removed.
  Remember:
  – You need to devise a fair test for each stain,
  – Removing the stain and ruining the sofa is not much use.

Here are some supposedly helpful hints on cleaning:

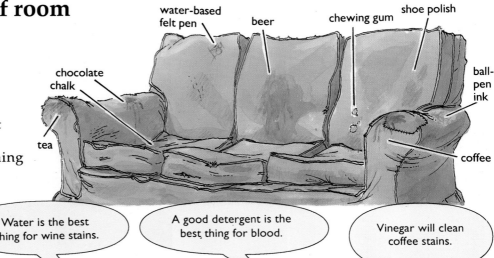

Some washing powders can fix some stains and make them more difficult to remove.

Water is the best thing for wine stains.

A good detergent is the best thing for blood.

Vinegar will clean coffee stains.

You can clean off chewing gum by freezing it with ice.

A solvent like ethanol will take off ball-pen ink.

EXTRAS

Planning

1 Does a solid dissolve faster if:
  – it is a powder or in lumps?
  – the solvent is hot?
  – there is more solvent?
  – the solvent is stirred?
  Which is most important?
  Design an investigation to find out which has the biggest effect on how fast something dissolves. You may be able to try out your plan using water as the solvent and sugar as the solute.

2 (a) Some mascaras are waterproof. What does this mean? Test some to see if they really are waterproof.
(b) Why are waterproof mascaras useful?
(c) Find a way of cleaning waterproof mascara smudges from a white collar.

15.12 Using reactions: enzymes

Recycling the silver

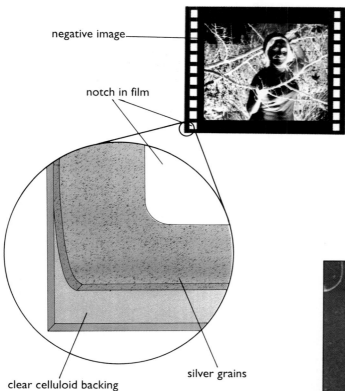

negative image

notch in film

clear celluloid backing

silver grains

Black and white photographic film uses compounds of silver that react to light. When light falls on them, they start to change from a compound to a lump of silver. This silver looks black. Photographers use chemicals called developers to speed up the process.

Film has two layers. The back layer is celluloid. It makes the film tough but flexible. The layer with the silver is called the emulsion. The silver salts are mixed with a protein called gelatin to stick them to the celluloid backing.

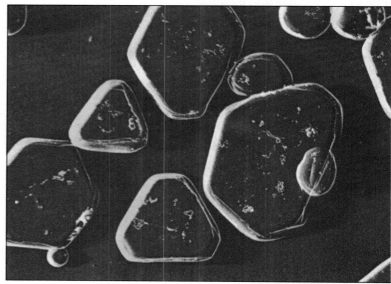

Silver bromide crystals on unexposed black and white film

Investigating

Using an enzyme

The silver in a negative can be recovered and used to make more film. The gelatin that is gluing it to the celluloid must be dissolved. The silver grains then fall away from the celluloid. Dissolving the gelatin is easy using an enzyme.

An enzyme is a complex chemical that can speed up a reaction. Enzymes can be used more than once.

● Design and carry out an investigation to answer one of these questions.

1 Does acid or alkali help the reaction?
2 What effect does temperature have?
3 Which has a bigger effect on the reaction: the temperature or the number of times that the enzyme has been used before?

Distillation

The town of Bushmills in Northern Ireland has the world's oldest licensed whiskey distillery. Whiskey had been made for many years in Bushmills when in 1608 Sir Thomas Philips was granted a licence to distil whiskey by James I of England. Bushmills is very well placed for a whiskey distillery. It has fields of barley growing all round it. Water from the local river, the Bush, is particularly clean and large supplies of peat for fuel are found locally.

1 Barley grains germinate in the malting. The barley produces enzymes which convert the insoluble starch in the seeds into sugars which can dissolve in water. The seed is then killed by gentle heating to stop the sugars from being used up. Hot water is added and the mixture, called mash, is allowed to stand.

Mash tubs at Bushmills distillery

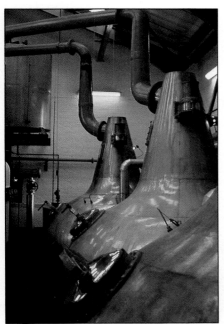

A copper still at Bushmills distillery

2 After about eight hours, the liquid is drained off and cooled. Yeast is added to ferment the sugar to alcohol. Fermentation takes about three days.

3 The yeast is removed from the liquid after fermentation. The liquid then goes to the still. The still heats it to give off vapours of alcohol and water. Alcohol boils at a lower temperature than water, so more alcohol is given off. This is the first distillation. Two more distillations produce a distillate that contains more and more alcohol.

4 At the end of the third distillation, pure water is added to reduce the strength of the liquid. It is then put into barrels and left to mature. This can take up to ten years.

5 When mature, whiskies are carefully blended. This involves mixing different types together to give just the right taste. After the blending is completed, the whiskey is bottled.

Investigating

What gives the most alcohol?

● The amount of carbon dioxide that the yeast gives off tells you how quickly the fermentation is going. Plan an investigation to find out the best conditions for making alcohol by fermentation.
You will need to think about:

– Is the amount of yeast important?
– How does adding more sugar affect the result?
– Is a longer, cooler fermentation better than a shorter, warmer one?

Get your plan checked by your teacher and then carry it out.

EXTRAS

1 Make a flow chart to show how whiskey is made. How many mixing and separating processes can you find?

2 What is the best way of getting alcohol from the mixture made by fermentation? Plan an investigation to find out if a fast distillation at a high temperature is better than a slow distillation at a lower temperature.

16 CONTROL

16·1 Setting the scene

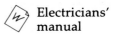

Lights

You are doing the lights for a school play. The play needs some special effects. You have been asked to design and build the circuits. You will need:
- two bright lights,
- two dim lights,
- one green spotlight that can follow someone on the stage.

You must be able to switch from the bright lights to the dim lights instantly.

● Make a model of a suitable system.

Standard circuit symbols

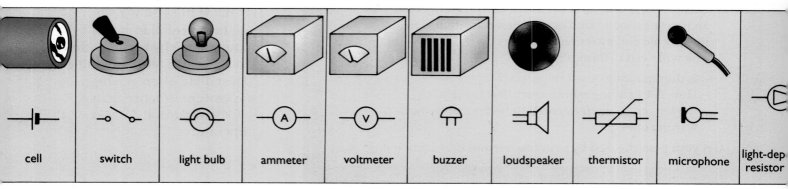

cell	switch	light bulb	ammeter	voltmeter	buzzer	loudspeaker	thermistor	microphone	light-dep resistor

Electrical circuits

Electricians use diagrams to describe their circuits. The key on page 74 shows the symbols for the different components.

Electricity can only flow through materials which conduct. When conductors join one end of a battery to the other end, electricity can flow. The route the electricity takes is called a circuit.

Electricity cannot flow if the circuit is not complete. A switch is a device that makes a gap in a circuit and stops the flow of electricity.

Flowing electricity carries energy which can do jobs like lighting bulbs.

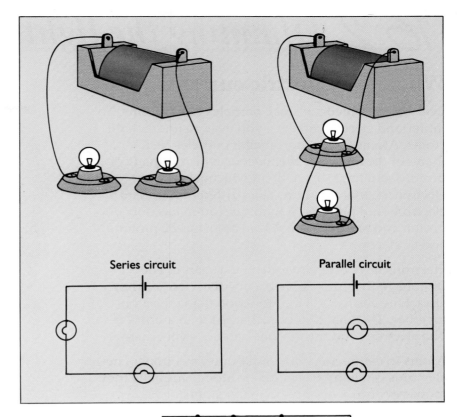

Series circuit

Parallel circuit

1 These street lights are in a parallel circuit. Why is this better than using a series circuit?

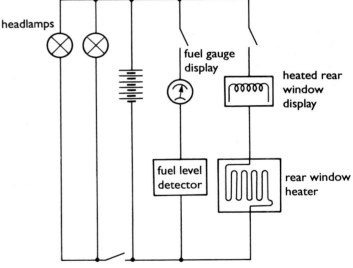

headlamps

fuel gauge display

heated rear window display

fuel level detector

rear window heater

This circuit diagram is part of a car.

2 Look at the part which makes the headlamps work. Is it series or parallel?

3 Copy the circuit that works the rear window heater. Is it series or parallel?

EXTRAS

1 Try to build some of the circuits shown on this page. What do they do? Now experiment with some of your own.

2 Design a lighting scheme for your bedroom. Which areas need most light? Which can be dimly lit? Draw a plan showing the lights you would use and where you would put them.

3 The same scene lit from different angles can look very different. Design and build a model stage set to try out various lighting effects.

16.2 Dimming the lights

What is an electric current?

Everything is made of small particles called atoms. To undertand electric currents, you need to understand atoms. Atoms have other smaller particles inside them. In the middle is the nucleus which is made of protons and neutrons. Outside the nucleus are electrons. Different atoms have different numbers of electrons and protons. A hydrogen atom has only one proton and one electron. A lead atom has 82 protons and 82 electrons.

Electrons have a negative electrical charge. The protons in the nucleus have a positive charge. They attract the electrons. This attraction holds the atom together. The total electrical charge for an atom is zero. The electrons and the protons balance each other.

Atoms in conductors have loose outer electrons. These electrons can jump from atom to atom. Normally they move very quickly between many atoms.

When a battery is connected in a circuit, the electrons tend to move in one direction. This flow of electrons is an electric current. Chemical reactions in a battery push electrons towards the negative end. This means the two terminals of the battery have different numbers of electrons. This difference is called a potential difference. It is measured in volts.

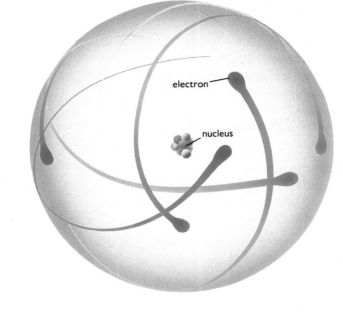

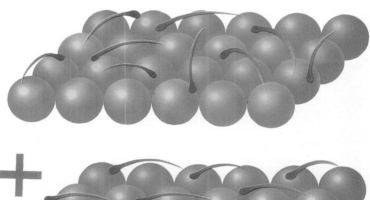

The electrons flow to remove these differences. The chemical reactions that cause the difference do not last for ever. Eventually the chemicals run out and the reaction stops. The battery has run down and the electrons in the wire move about freely again.

Investigating

How easily does electricity flow?

At the end of the second scene you have to dim the lights. This lets the stage hands change the props without closing the curtains.

● Design and carry out investigations to answer these questions:
  – Do copper wires carry electricity more easily than steel wires?
  – Which has a bigger effect on the amount of electricity flowing through a wire – its length or its thickness?
● Use your answers to design and make a safe, effective dimmer switch.

Conductors

A conductor that lets electrons pass easily has a low resistance. Superconductors are substances that allow electrons to flow with almost no resistance.

Insulators

An insulator has a high resistance. Insulators have electrons which are tightly bound into the atoms. They cannot move between atoms, so no current can flow.

Communicating

Using a model

The explanation of electric current is a scientific model. It is one way of explaining what we observe about electricity. Use this model to explain the results from your investigation about how easily electricity flows. Diagrams might help.

EXTRAS

1 A bulb glows when electricity passes through it. Make a list of other things that electricity can do to things through which it passes.

2 Extractor fans for shops and buildings need to be controlled. If they run too slowly, the air inside gets stuffy. If they run too fast, the air gets too cold. Build a circuit which controls how fast a fan turns. You can use a small motor and a cardboard fan. Find a way to measure how fast the fan turns. How does the voltage used affect how quickly the fan turns?

Observing

3 Build the circuit shown on the right and get it checked by your teacher. Stretch a piece of steel wool between the crocodile clips and switch on. Note what happens. Try again with a shorter wire. Explain what you see happening.

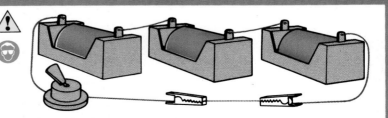

16·3 Magnets

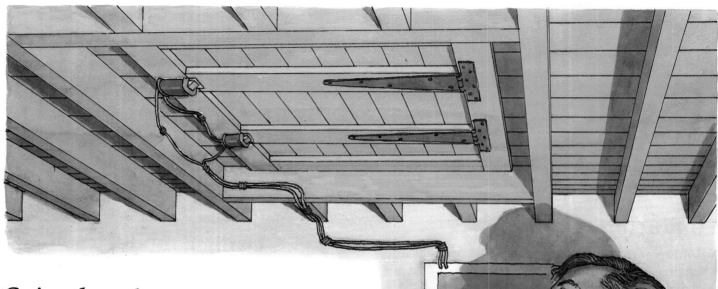

Going down!

In one scene an actor has to disappear into the ground! This can be done using a trap door in the stage floor.

● Design and build a trapdoor. It must have a bolt that can be operated from the off-stage lighting control room. Use the diagrams on these pages to help you.

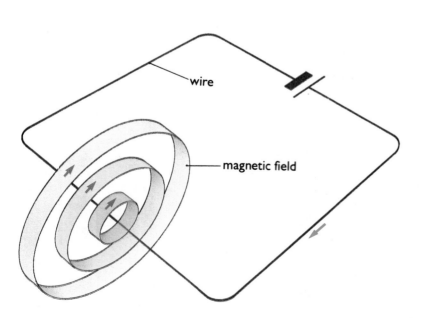

wire

magnetic field

Magnetic fields

When an electric current flows along a wire, the current makes a magnetic field round it. This field is like the field round a magnet. Look at the diagram on the left and those on the top of page 79. The blue arrows show the direction of the electric current. The red arrows show the direction of the magnetic lines of force. The closer the red lines, the stronger the magnetic field.

The magnetic field is affected by:
- the current,
- the direction of the current,
- any other magnetic fields near it,
- the material inside the coil.

The diagrams below show magnetic fields round a coil of wire (called a solenoid) and a bar magnet. A solenoid is like a magnet that can be switched on and off.

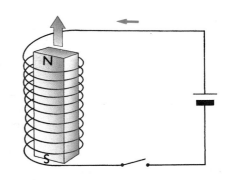

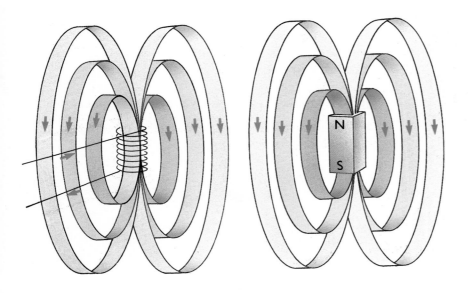

Magnets can attract or repel each other. When current is flowing through a solenoid, the solenoid acts like a magnet. It can repel or attract another solenoid or a magnet. It can also attract (but not repel) a piece of unmagnetised iron or steel. You can use this idea to make a bolt which can be opened by an electric current.

Hi-fi speakers – from current to movement

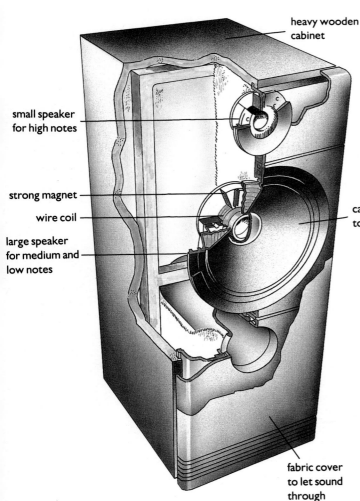

heavy wooden cabinet

small speaker for high notes

strong magnet

wire coil

large speaker for medium and low notes

cardboard cone to make sound waves

fabric cover to let sound through

Loudspeakers use a coil of wire which hangs between the poles of a strong magnet. When an electric current flows through the coil, the coil starts to move. The way it moves depends on how electricity flows through it. The coil is attached to a cone-shaped piece of cardboard which moves in and out. This makes sound waves in the air.

Magnetic tapes and computer discs can be demagnetised by powerful electromagnets.

EXTRAS

1 Look carefully at a real moving-coil loudspeaker. Which parts are magnetic? Why do they need to be magnetic?

Planning

2 Plan some tests to see how close a cassette tape can be to a loudspeaker before the recording on the tape is damaged.

16·4 Alarms

A door alarm system

Some people are sneaking in to see the play without paying. You think they may be coming in through a fire door.

1 Why must fire doors always be left unlocked?

● Design an alarm system that tells you when a fire door is opened.

A magnet detector

Opera glasses are supplied for the audience. Unfortunately, people tend to take them home. How can you tell if anyone is carrying one of these sets of glasses in their pocket or bag?

One possibility is to use a magnet detector. A magnet is surrounded by a magnetic field. If a wire is moved through this field, an electric current starts to flow along the wire.

This effect can be used to detect magnets. A coil of wire connected to a sensitive meter will show a small current when a magnet is moved near it.

The further away the magnet, the weaker the fields become. Larger coils with more windings of wire are needed to detect very weak magnetic fields.

● Design a security system to stop people taking the glasses out of the hall.

Books in this library have tiny magnets hidden in them. If someone takes a book between the two coils, an alarm will sound.

X-rays are used at airports to look into suitcases and bags. Why are they not used for people?

Hi-fi cartridges – from movement to current

A record has a wobbly, spiral groove running from the edge to the middle. This groove is specially cut in the factory. Its wobble has the same pattern of peaks and troughs as the original sound.

The needle of a cartridge travels along this groove as the record turns. This makes the needle wobble and move a tiny coil of wire in a magnetic field. An electric current flows in the coil.

An amplifier converts the small current from the cartridge into a larger current with the same pattern. This drives the loudspeakers; they convert the electrical energy back into sound waves.

Most modern cartridges use special crystals which make electricity when they are stretched or crushed. They are called piezoelectric crystals. The groove on the record controls how the crystal moves.

EXTRAS

1 A generator is a machine that changes movement into electricity. It uses coils and magnets. Draw a design for a generator that would produce the most electricity from a small movement.

2 How can you detect a magnet that is not moving? Design a machine to solve this problem.

16·5 Paying the bills

An electric shock?

The school charges the show's producer for all electricity used during the performance. Make a list of all the things that use electricity. Include heating and lighting for the school hall.

The bill was far more than the producer had expected. She needs to save a lot of money, or the whole production will make a loss. She has made a list of all of the things she can think of that use electricity.

1 Has she missed anything?
2 How could she make savings?

List made by the show's producer

Appliance	What is it used for?	Rating	How long is it on?
space heater	heating hall during play	5000 W	3 h
main spotlight	lighting effects	1500 W	30 min
flood lights	lighting effects	2000 W	1 h 40 min
sound system	sound effects	200 W	1 h 50 min
trapdoor	special effects	300 W	15 s
security system	preventing theft from hall	10 W	2 h
ventilation fan	cooling stage area	1000 W	1 h 40 min
emergency lighting	lighting in case of power failure	250 W	uses battery
water boiler	making tea and coffee at the interval	2500 W	30 min

Energy supplied

When you pay for electricity, you pay for energy. The amount of electrical energy depends on two things:
– how much energy each electron carries,
– how many electrons flow every second.

The energy one electron carries is very small. Billions of electrons need to flow before we can detect even a very small flow of energy. The energy each electron carries depends on how much push it has been given by the battery. This push can be measured in volts.

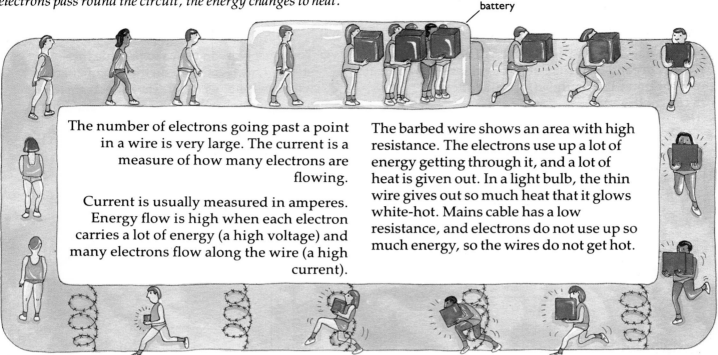

The runners on the track are a picture of electrons in a circuit. The battery uses chemical reactions to supply electrons with energy, shown as red cubes. As the electrons pass round the circuit, the energy changes to heat.

battery

The number of electrons going past a point in a wire is very large. The current is a measure of how many electrons are flowing.

Current is usually measured in amperes. Energy flow is high when each electron carries a lot of energy (a high voltage) and many electrons flow along the wire (a high current).

The barbed wire shows an area with high resistance. The electrons use up a lot of energy getting through it, and a lot of heat is given out. In a light bulb, the thin wire gives out so much heat that it glows white-hot. Mains cable has a low resistance, and electrons do not use up so much energy, so the wires do not get hot.

Energy used

An electricity bill tells you how much energy you have used. The total energy depends on:
- the energy each electron carries (the voltage),
- how many electrons flow (the current).
- how long the electrons flow for (the time).

electrical energy = current × voltage × time

With mains electricity:
- the voltage is 240 volt,
- the current depends on the appliance (heaters and cookers use a lot, lights and TVs use less),
- the time is how long you leave the appliance on.

Electrical power is how fast you use energy. It is measure in watts:

electrical power = current × voltage

As 1 watt is only a small amount of power, a kilowatt is often used. This is 1000 watts.

The unit on an electricity bill is the energy needed to provide 1 kilowatt of power for 1 hour.

Look at the electricity bill.
3 What is the price per unit?
4 How many units have been used?
5 What will the total cost be?

East Midlands Electricity

MRS S PATRICK
12 MARIGHELA RD
MEASLING
MG3 4FB

IN ALL COMMUNICATIONS PLEASE QUOTE

Customer Reference Number	Date of Account
91 64 300220 59	16 DEC 90

FOR ENQUIRIES ABOUT THIS ACCOUNT PLEASE RING YOUR DISTRICT OFFICE IMMEDIATELY (MON-FRI 9.00 a.m. –4.30 p.m.)

Tel. No. MEASLING 757119

R

SEE OVERLEAF FOR WAYS TO PAY AND EASY PAYMENT METHODS INCLUDING THE PAYMENT OF THIS BILL BY A BUDGET ACCOUNT.

METER READINGS		Tariff Code	UNITS	PENCE PER UNIT	AMOUNT EXCLUSIVE OF TAX	VAT REG No. 138267911	
Present	Previous					Tax	% Rate
85991	85110	10	881	7.000	61.67		
		STANDING CHARGE – SEE OVERLEAF			7.33		
		TOTAL ENERGY CHARGE			69.00	0.00	0.00

PLEASE QUOTE YOUR CUSTOMER REFERENCE NUMBER IF YOU NEED TO CONTACT US REGARDING THIS BILL. WHY NOT PAY THIS AND FUTURE BILLS BY DIRECT DEBIT. TO JOIN THIS SCHEME PLEASE COMPLETE AND RETURN THE MANDATE OVERLEAF

TARIFF CODE		
10 DOMESTIC	69.00	0.00

PROGRAMMED READING DATE	THIS AMOUNT (incl. tax) IS NOW DUE
16 DEC 90	**£** 69.00 Please pay before 30 DEC 90

The standing charge pays the rent on the electricity meter

EXTRAS

1 If electricity costs 7p per unit (1 kilowatt hour), how much did the heating for the school play cost?

2 Iceco Ltd have developed a new type of fridge. It uses half the power of a normal fridge. Iceco plan to sell their energy-efficient fridge for £150. A normal fridge of this size would cost £105 and use 0.85 units every day. How long would it take before the Iceco fridge started to save its owner money?

Sights and sounds

The play uses lots of special effects. These need to be carefully organised if they are to work properly and at the right time. The sound effects include:
- a clap of thunder,
- the sound of wind,
- voices off stage (some distorted),
- the sound of a small battle (knights on horseback).

The visual effects include:
- a sunset,
- a dream scene,
- flashes of lightning,
- a ghost.

- You must work in teams to provide these effects. One team must do the sound effects with a cassette recorder. The other team must do the lighting effects using lamps and filters.
- When you are all ready, have an 'effects rehearsal'. Try to get everything to work in the right order and at the right time.

Analogue recording

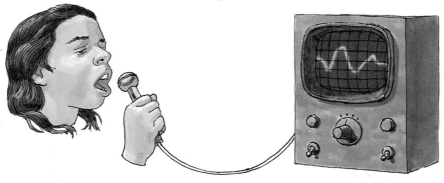

Sound can be recorded as electrical signals in two ways: analogue and digital. Analogue recording makes an electrical pattern that is the same shape as the original sound waves. This means that high-frequency sound will give a high-frequency pattern. The electrical pattern is called the signal.

player

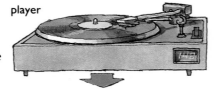

amplifier

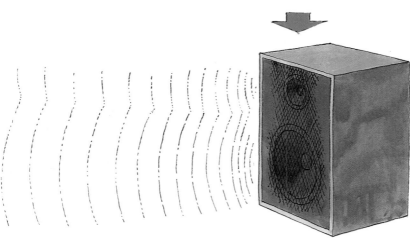

Electrical equipment is not perfect. It adds crackles and hisses to the signal which you can hear on tape recorders or record players. This is often called noise. It comes from faults in the electrical machines and problems with the medium which is being used to store the signal. For example, magnetic tape tends to have a slight hiss. You can hear this if you turn up the volume when you play a blank tape in a cassette recorder.

Electronic engineers have tried to design filters to remove this noise from the signal. This is very difficult, because the noise and the signal look very similar.

Digital recording

Digital recording uses a different system for coding and storing the signal. It splits each part of the music up into tiny bits. These bits describe the shape of the original sound signal but do not look like it. These bits can be stored in a simple ON–OFF code.

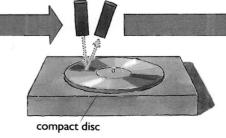

laser   detector

compact disc

Compact discs contain millions of these little ON–OFF signals on their surface. The signals are read by a sensor as the disc spins round in the player. A small microprocessor in the player then rebuilds the original electrical signal. It can be sent to the loudspeakers and converted into sound waves.

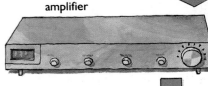

amplifier

The electrical equipment still adds noise to the signal. But noise is an analogue signal. It is very different from the digital music signal and the two can easily be separated. Compact discs are also much tougher than plastic records and tapes.

EXTRAS

1 Compare the price of tapes, records and compact discs. Which is the best value for money? You could do a survey to find out what other people think.

2 Prepare a report that compares some electrical appliances. Choose something you know about and can test – perhaps personal stereos or radios. Design your tests carefully to make sure they are fair.

Your report should give the good and bad points about each appliance you tested. Then pick:
– your 'best buy',
– the machine that does the job better than any of the others.

3 With some friends, produce a short play on a model stage. Use as many effects as possible. You can write your own script or use a story you know.

Filled, capped and loaded

This system fills bottles at a brewery. Every bottle must be:
– filled to the right level,
– fitted with a cap,
– loaded into a crate.

Electronic devices monitor and control the production line.

A detector can tell whether a cap is fitted or not.

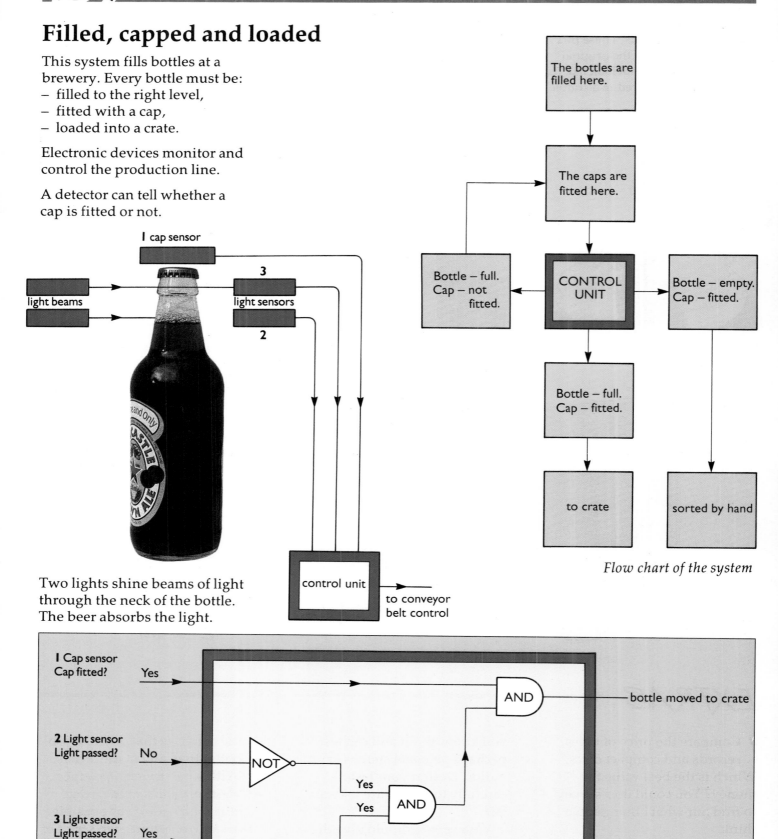

Two lights shine beams of light through the neck of the bottle. The beer absorbs the light.

Flow chart of the system

The logic circuit in the control unit

Logic gates

The control unit uses logic gates. There are three types of logic gates. They ask simple questions and produce an answer. YES means the sensor has been activated.

The AND gate
This needs two YES signals before it will give out a YES signal.

The NOT gate
This converts a YES into a NO, or a NO into a YES signal.

The OR gate
If either of the signals coming in is YES, it will give out a YES signal.

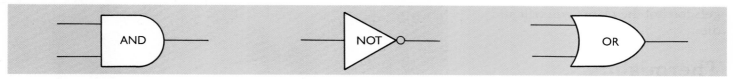

Full and empty bottles

- Design the logic system that would detect:
  - full bottles without caps,
  - empty bottles with caps.

1 The system does not need to detect full bottles with caps on. Why?

Relays

Logic gates need a low voltage supply to work properly. But the conveyor belt in the factory needs a powerful electric motor to work properly. This needs a lot of energy and a high voltage supply. The logic gates control the conveyor belt with a relay. This is a low-voltage device that can switch on the motor driving the conveyor belt.

2 What will happen when a small electric current flows through the coil in the relay? Why?

3 Connect a relay to a suitable battery and see what happens. Try it a few times.

4 What will happen when the current in the coil is switched off? Why?

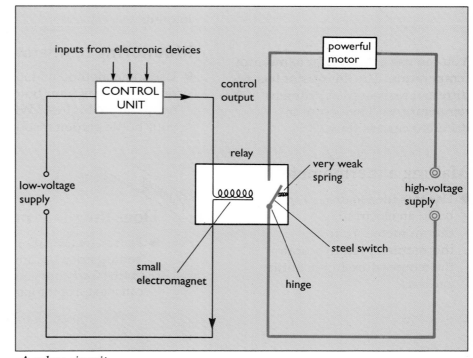

A relay circuit

EXTRAS

1 Design a fire warning system for a school. You can use six smoke detectors and a control box with logic gates. The system should:
- set off an alarm when any of the smoke detectors sends in a signal,
- have a panel which shows which detector has been set off,
- have a reset button to switch the system off.

2 Design a system with two buttons for a quiz show. Each contestant will have their own button and light. As soon as one button is pressed, its light must come on and it must stop any of the other buttons from working.

16·8 A bottle garden

A bottle garden is a very carefully balanced system. If it gets too wet, the sides mist up and you cannot see the plants. If it gets too dry, the plants die. There are similar problems with the temperature. If it gets too hot the plants will wilt and die.

Thermistors

A thermistor is a resistor whose resistance changes when its temperature changes. The symbol for a thermistor is:

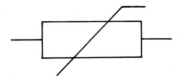

You can use a thermistor to monitor temperature. The thermistor has a different resistance at different temperatures. This means a different current flows.

Making a thermometer

- Use this idea to design and build an electronic thermometer. Your thermometer has to monitor the temperature in the bottle garden.

Data logging

If you connect an electronic thermometer to a computer, you can monitor the temperature over a long time. This is called data logging.

Monitoring temperature

- Use some method of data logging to see what happens to the temperature in your bottle garden on a typical day. When is the temperature highest? When is it lowest? How do the plants in your bottle garden respond to these changes in temperature?

Planning

Does the plant make a difference?

- Plan an investigation to find out if putting a plant in your bottle garden has any effect on the temperature inside the bottle. Carry out your investigation if you have time. You can make a bottle garden out of a clear plastic bottle.

EXTRAS

1 Build a battery-powered electronic thermometer. It should read temperatures in the range 0°C to 50°C.

2 Are all the parts of the bottle garden warming up and cooling down in the same way? Find some hot or cold spots.

3 Write down at least five possible uses for thermistors in your home.

16·9 Water probes

Most plants die very quickly without water. Many plants die from over-watering. They need to have just the right amount of water to stay green and growing.

Aaagh!

This circuit shows a simple water-sensitive switch. The gap between the two wires A and B is normally dry. Dry air has a very high resistance, so no current flows. When the wires are dipped in water, a current can flow. It is only a very small current because water is a poor conductor.

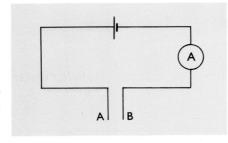

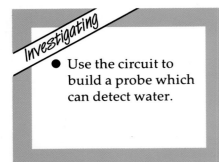

Investigating

● Use the circuit to build a probe which can detect water.

A suspect takes a lie-detector test

Some lie detectors measure the amount of moisture on the skin. Scientists say that when someone is lying they get nervous and sweat more. This makes the skin conduct electricity better. A sensitive meter can detect this change. But do people always sweat when they tell lies?

● Design an investigation to find out if liars do sweat more. Are there any other changes in their bodies?

EXTRAS

1 Use your probe to make a meter that makes a noise when the water falls below a safe level. In this way, the plant can ask you to water it when it is getting dry!

2 Electrodes used for picking up small electrical signals in the body have to be stuck on with jelly. What must this jelly be like? Make a list of the properties of the jelly. Try to find some substances that could do the job and test them to see which is best.

3 Does ice conduct electricity? Find out.

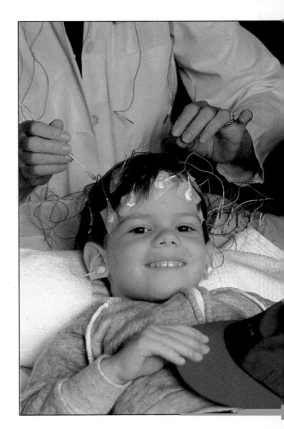

Fixing electrodes to a patient's forehead to measure electrical signals in the brain for an EEG (electroencephalograph) examination

A shark needs salt water, but this water would kill a brown trout

Investigating

Water for fish ⚠

Many zoos have collections of fish. Marine fish need to be kept in sea water, but other fish need fresh water. The supply of water in zoos must not get mixed up. Sea water would kill many river fish. The water going into a tank can be checked with electronic probes. If the type of water is wrong, an alarm will go off.

● Sea water has a much lower electrical resistance than fresh water. Use this fact to design a probe for detecting salt water. Build your probe and test it for reliability.

1 Can anything confuse your probe?

2 How dilute a solution of salt can it detect?

Pure water?

Deionised water is water containing no dissolved substances that conduct electricity. It is used in steam irons and chemical solutions.

Deionised water is made by passing tap water through chemicals that can remove dissolved substances.

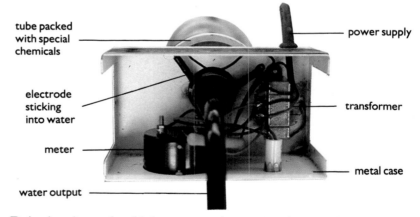

Deioniser in a school laboratory. This makes deionised water from tap water

EXTRAS

1 Use your probe to test different brands of bottled waters. Which are the purest? Are these the best brands?

2 What can you dissolve in water without affecting how easily it conducts electricity? Test as many things as you can. Are there any patterns?

16·11 Light work

Many houses have burglar alarms. They all work by detecting unexpected changes in the environment – for example:
– a light in a dark room,
– a sound in a room that should be empty and quiet,
– a movement in an empty room,
– the heat of a human body,
– the weight of someone walking across a hidden switch.

● Design a burglar alarm system for the room shown here. You could use two or three of the ideas above. For each part of your system, explain how you hope to detect any intruders. How would you turn the system on without setting the alarm ringing?

EXTRAS

1 LDRs can be used in circuits for street lamps. Design a circuit that turns on the main lamp when it starts to get dark.
2 How does an LDR circuit help to stop all the shopping falling off the end of a conveyor belt in the supermarket?

The arrow points to the LDR sensor

Investigating

Detecting light

A light-dependent resistor (usually called an LDR) detects changes in the level of light.
● Design and carry out an investigation to find out how light levels affect the resistance of an LDR.
● Build a circuit that will detect a burglar's torch in a dark office.
● Imagine you are a burglar. You know an office is equipped with an alarm system that can detect the light of a torch. Investigate the effect of changing the colour of the bulb in your torch. Can you find a colour of light that will let you see what you are doing but will not set off the alarm?

17 ENVIRONMENT
17·1 Soils

What sort of soil do plants need to grow?

Develop your own brand of potting compost. Use some of the things shown. You will need to:

● design tests to find which compost gives the best growth of plants,
● work out the costs of your compost.

It will take a while to get all your results, so be patient.

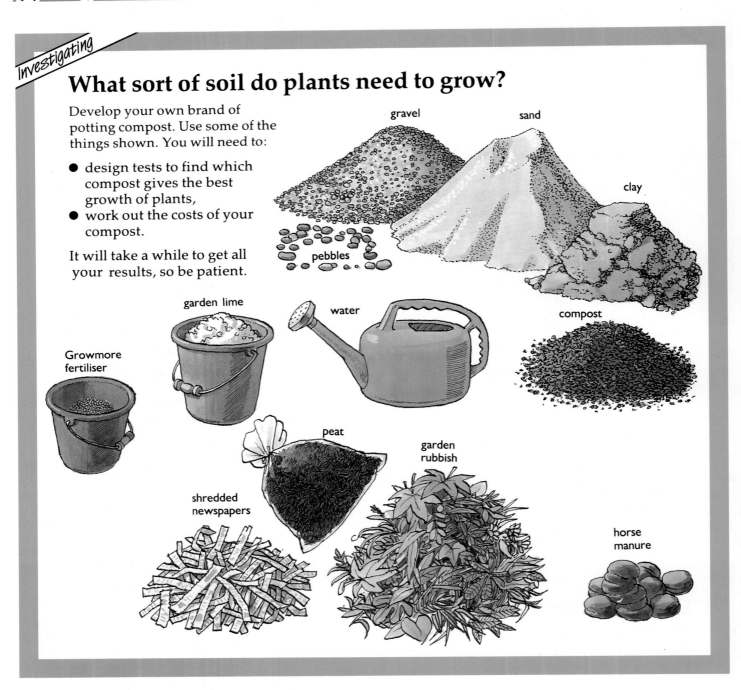

gravel

sand

clay

pebbles

garden lime

water

compost

Growmore fertiliser

peat

garden rubbish

shredded newspapers

horse manure

What does good soil contain? ⚠ 📝

Test some soil samples.

● Take some samples from areas that you think are very good for plants – perhaps a field or a small woodland.
● Take other samples from areas that have very little plant growth – maybe a piece of waste ground near a factory.

1 Can you find any differences between the soils?

How is soil made?

Soil takes a very long time to form. Charles Darwin worked out it could take 100 years to make just 10 cm of topsoil.

First, rocks and stones break down into smaller bits. Part of this job is done by plants and animals. When they die, their bodies decay. This makes a black, sticky substance called humus. Humus mixes with the bits of rock to make something like soil.

Soon, larger plants and animals make their home in it. Their growing roots or moving bodies mix the soil together. They also help to mix air into the soil.

Planning

Worms in the soil

Earthworms are some of the most important animals for making soil. Plan an investigation to look at one of the questions below.

2 What do worms eat?
3 Do worms prefer (a) fresh, green leaves or (b) dry, brown leaves?
4 Do worms burrow deeper into the ground in hot weather?
5 Can worms tell light from dark? If so, can they see different colours?

Observing

Layers in the soil

Soils have different layers. The top layers are usually the most fertile. They contain the humus and a good supply of air. The humus breaks down slowly to give out minerals. The lower layers are made of rocks and stones that have not been broken down.

Small plants (like grass) have roots that grow in the top layers. These roots quickly absorb minerals and water. Even the roots of large trees, like oak and pine, are mainly in the top layers. This means there is strong competition for water and minerals here. Trees also have much bigger roots which pass down into lower levels. They can absorb minerals and water and bring them to the surface.

6 What do you notice about the way the soil changes as it gets deeper?
7 The orangish layer is clay and gravel. Give two differences between this and the top layer.
8 Write down two ways that minerals in the lower clay layers get into the top layer.
9 Ploughing turns the soil layer over. Why is it not a good idea to plough too deeply?

Soil profile – sandy loam over pale clay and gravel

EXTRAS

1 (a) Design a test to see how quickly water can drain through a soil sample.
(b) Find out if plants grow better in a fast-draining or a slow-draining compost.
   Try some of these tests on your potting compost.

2 Your teacher will give you some sterilised soil. Design an investigation to see if sterile or normal soil is better for growing seeds. If you get time, carry out your plan.

3 Sprinkle a dilute solution of washing-up liquid in water on to some soil. Earthworms will come to the surface. Work out how many earthworms live under your lawn or the school playing field. But don't cover it all with washing-up liquid!

17·2 Keeping it green

Rainforests

Look at the photographs. They were all taken in the same area.

- Decide which photograph was taken first.
- Put the others in the order in which they were taken. What clues can you use to decide on the right order?
- Make a list of all the changes you can see between the first and last photos.
- Which of these changes would be most difficult to undo?

The rainforests are some of the most productive areas of land in the world. Thousands of types of plants and animals live on every square kilometre.

- Write down a list of reasons why burning the rainforests is a bad idea. Why do people do it?

What keeps soil fertile?

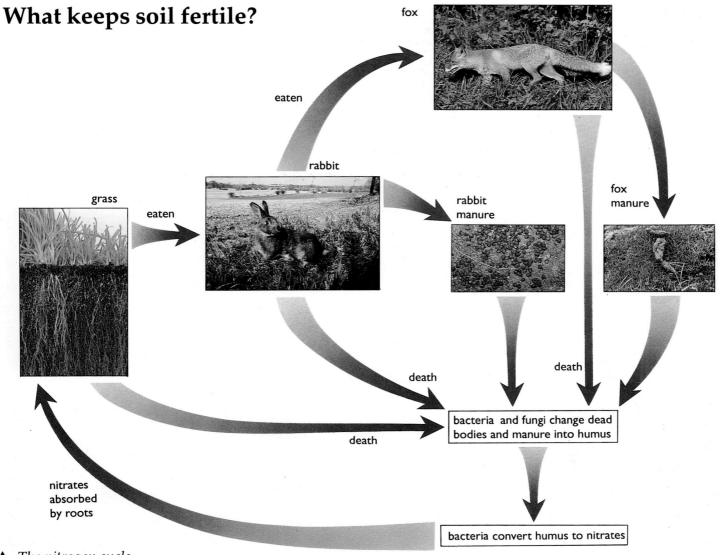

▲ *The nitrogen cycle*

1 Which of these things will help the cycle shown above:
  – ploughing weeds back into the soil after harvest?
  – spreading muck from a cow shed over grassland?
  – putting all the weeds from a day's gardening in the dustbin?
  – mowing the lawn and composting the clippings?

2 Sometimes we remove plants for food. How does this affect the soil fertility?

3 How can farmers help to keep their soils fertile if plants are removed for food?

EXTRAS

1 What is a fertiliser? What do we need to make it?

2 Can you tell the difference between 'organic' crops (grown without artificial fertilisers) and other crops? Design a test and try it out if you can.

Planning

3 Fertilisers are very expensive. Design an investigation to find out:
  (a) how much fertiliser you need to use,
  (b) the best time to add it to the soil.

17·3 Soil erosion

Soil is a complicated mixture of different things loosely held together.
If it is broken apart, it may be too badly damaged to recover.

Investigating

Erosion by running water

One of the things that can damage soil is
running water. Soil can be washed from the
sides of mountains and end up clogging the
rivers in the valleys.

Investigate some of the questions below.

1 Does bare soil erode more quickly than soil
with plants on it?
2 Which produces more erosion: a small
stream flowing for a long time or the same
amount of water in a quick flood?
3 Which has the greater effect on erosion:
the amount of water or the steepness
of the slope?
4 What else might affect the rate of
erosion of a soil?

Use the results from your investigations to prepare a plan for the
farmers in Arapo Valley in California. Your plan needs to explain:
– how erosion is caused,
– which areas of the valley are most likely to suffer from erosion,
– how the farmers should try to prevent it from happening.

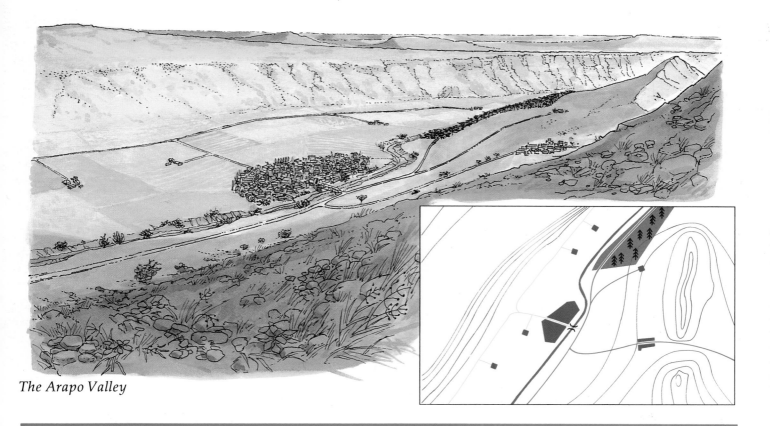

The Arapo Valley

Wind erosion

Dust storm in Kansas

Another thing that can cause soil erosion is wind. This is a particular problem in East Anglia. Flat ground stretching for kilometres in every direction allows strong winds to blow dry, powdery soil from one field to another. This is made worse when farmers clear hedgerows to make bigger fields from a lot of small ones.

Planning

Windbreaks

Plan an investigation to answer one of these questions:

5 Does the height of a windbreak affect how well it works?

6 Which work better – solid walls or fences with gaps?

EXTRAS

1 Design a scarecrow that moves to scare birds in even the slightest wind. It must be strong enough to withstand strong gales as well. Plan an investigation to test how effective it is at scaring birds.

2 Which countries are most likely to suffer from soil erosion? Use a library to find out where soil erosion has done the most damage. What can be done to prevent it getting worse?

3 Do sandy soils erode more quickly than humus-rich soils? Design an investigation to find out. If you have time, try it out.

17·4 Weather

Local weather

- Do a survey of your school (or home) to find out what weather conditions are like in different parts of the grounds (or garden). Before you start, think carefully.

1 What will you measure, and why:
  - rainfall?
  - wind speed and direction?
  - temperature?

2 How will you take measurements? This page might give you some clues.

3 How will you record your results? What do you need to note down?

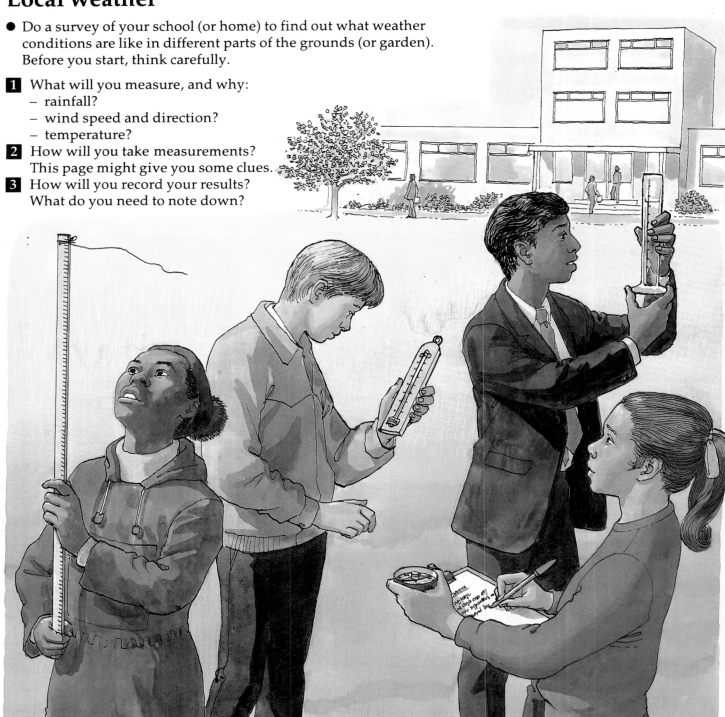

- When you have collected your results, work with other groups in your class to produce a whole school map. This should show different classrooms, playgrounds and so on. Plot on the map the things you have measured.

4 Can you see any surprisingly cold areas? Or warm spots? Where is it most windy?

- Use your map to suggest where you should put
  - a windmill,
  - a garden of sunflowers,
  - a weather station to take readings for the whole area,
  - a garden with wetland plants like reeds and mosses,
  - a greenhouse.

Controlling the weather

We cannot really control the weather. The best we can do is to build homes and control the conditions inside.

Plants can also be protected from harsh conditions. A greenhouse allows plants to grow slightly earlier than they could outside.

- You can make cheap mini-greenhouses from plastic bottles. Design a fair test to see if the colour of the bottle has any effect.

5 Which colour bottle is best for plants?

6 What else might affect the growth of the plants?

If you have time, carry out your test.

Plastic mini-greenhouses

Wind and rain

Winds blow away from the centre of an area of high pressure towards the middle of a depression (an area of low pressure). However, because the Earth is turning, the winds do not blow straight from high pressure to low. In the northern hemisphere, they blow in a clockwise spiral away from high pressure, and they blow in an anticlockwise spiral towards the centre of a depression.

The air the wind brings can be wet or dry. If the air has come over the ocean, it is likely to be wet, and that usually means rain.

⌇ lines of equal air pressure

→ wind direction

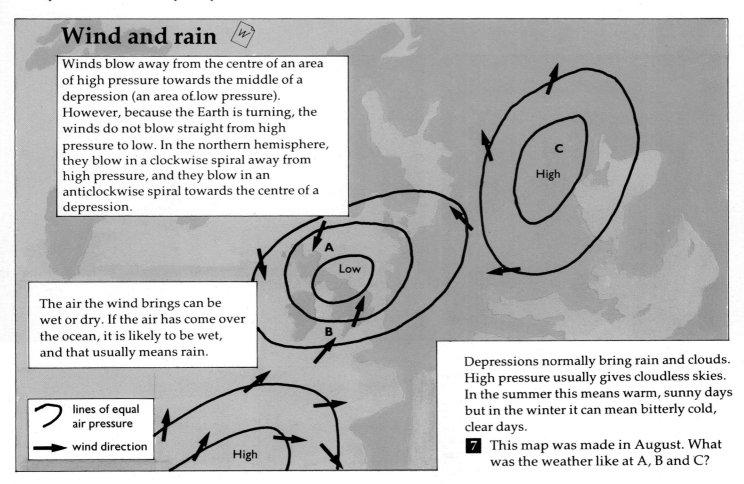

Depressions normally bring rain and clouds. High pressure usually gives cloudless skies. In the summer this means warm, sunny days but in the winter it can mean bitterly cold, clear days.

7 This map was made in August. What was the weather like at A, B and C?

EXTRAS

1 In the winter of 1989-90, Britain was buffeted by storms. Strong winds did millions of pounds' worth of damage. Look around at your home for things that could be easily damaged by strong winds. Roof tiles, greenhouses and garden sheds were badly hit. Suggest ways of protecting these against strong winds.

2 Windmills have to face into the wind. Design a windmill that automatically turns to face the direction from which the wind is coming.

17·5 Wetlands

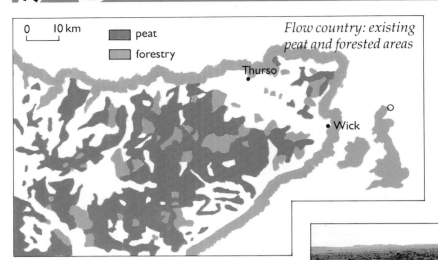

Flow country: existing peat and forested areas

- peat
- forestry

0 10 km

Thurso

Wick

Wetlands with waterlogged soils are not often used for agriculture. They cannot grow much that is useful. However, modern machines are able to cut drainage channels through the soil. Other plants can then be grown. In the north of Scotland, large areas of drained wetlands are being planted with conifers. Conservationists say this is a disaster. Foresters say it is simply a matter of exploiting available resources. What do you think?

Flow country

Ploughing for forestry

Mature Sitka spruce

Planning

The changing landscape

The changes in the landscape are enormous. But can they be measured?

- Plan a system to measure important changes over ten years. You will need to decide:
  - what should be measured about the soil,
  - what should be measured about the animals and plants living in the area,
  - any other things that need to be monitored.

In your plan explain exactly how you will measure one of the important changes you have mentioned.

Soil is a mixture of many different things. One of the most important is air. The roots of plants need oxygen to grow. If the soil is completely waterlogged, the roots are starved of oxygen.

When no air can get to the soil, dead plants and animals only decay slowly. If the dead bodies do not decay, an important link in the nitrogen cycle is broken. Swamp plants often lack nitrogen and other minerals.

To drain or not to drain?

The flow country is an area of wetland in the north of Scotland. In 1987, the Highland Regional Council set up a committee to decide the best thing to do with the flow country. Some of the evidence for and against development is given on the worksheet.

The natural habitat is:
– a home for scarce carnivorous plants,

– a nesting place for rare birds,

– a sporting venue (for some people).

Greater butterwort

Golden plover

Grouse shooting

Redevelopment provides:
– a managed, renewable natural resource,

– valuable manufacturing industry.

Timber from drained land

Scottish paper

● Write a paragraph for and against each of these uses of wild country.

EXTRAS

1 Design a test to compare how different plants stand up to being waterlogged.

2 Swamps and marshes often produce methane gas. This is made when bacteria break down dead plants and animals. These bacteria are able to live without much oxygen. Design a machine to convert waste organic materials (say sewage) into useful methane.

Investigating

3 Are there any other ways to stop soils becoming waterlogged? Think of as many ways as you can. Design a fair test to compare your ideas. Before you start you will need to think about how to measure:
– the amount of water in a soil sample,
– how quickly water drains from a soil sample.
Get your ideas checked by your teacher.
If you have time, carry out your tests.

17·6 Badlands

The Badlands are an area in the United States where the soil has been damaged so much that the ground has become a desert. The photographs on this page all show damaged land.

1 What has caused the damage in each photo?

2 What things can be done to improve the land.

◀ *Zabriskie Point, California*

China clay mining in Cornwall

A landfill rubbish site

City land

Land in cities is very expensive. In some parts of London, land can cost 100 times more than a similar plot on the west coast of Scotland.

Many cities have large amounts of damaged or derelict land. Some of these derelict areas are being improved and brought back into use.

3 What are the advantages of reusing derelict land?

Poisoned land

One of the main problems facing modern developers is that some of the derelict land has been poisoned. In the past, factories caused a lot of pollution. The chemicals left by these factories are called pollutants. Pollutants containing lead and copper can often be found on the sites of old metalworks. The usual way to deal with this problem is to carry all the poisoned soil away. Other bits of rubbish (old buildings, machinery and so on) also need to be cleared away. This is very expensive.

4 What other problems are caused by moving the soil away?

5 Scientists are often asked to work out how much soil needs to be moved. The developers will want to move the smallest possible amount. Why is this?

6 What might happen if clean soil is laid on top of poisoned soils?

Top: Albert Dock, Liverpool – derelict

Bottom: Albert Dock after redevelopment

Investigating

Copper pollution ⚠️ 🥽

Design an investigation into the effects of copper pollution on plant growth. Get your plans checked by your teacher. Then, carry them out. You can use copper sulphate solution to act as copper pollution in your tests.

7 How much copper can plants survive?

8 Do all plants react to copper in the same way?

9 Does the acidity of the soil make any difference?

EXTRAS

1 Do a survey of your local area. Can you find any derelict land? What do you think it should be used for? Give reasons for your choices.

2 Areas of water are often derelict. How can these be improved? How will the treatment for a canal differ from the treatment for land?

17·7 Round the bend

What is the greatest human invention? Is it the wheel? The printing press? The computer? The space shuttle? The flush toilet?

How good is a modern toilet? Can the design be improved? Clivus is one alternative.

- Compare a flush toilet with a Clivus.
- Prepare an advertisement for each type. Make sure you stress the good points of each design.

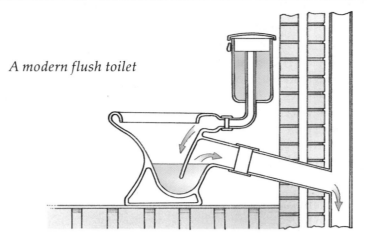

A modern flush toilet

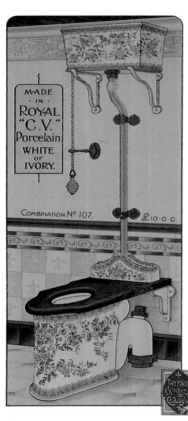

◄ *Victorian flush toilet*

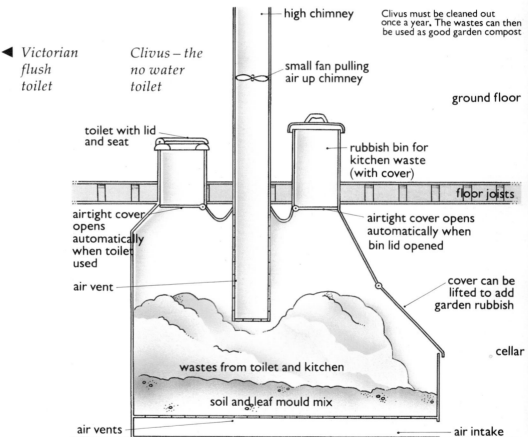

Clivus – the no water toilet

high chimney

Clivus must be cleaned out once a year. The wastes can then be used as good garden compost

small fan pulling air up chimney

ground floor

toilet with lid and seat

rubbish bin for kitchen waste (with cover)

airtight cover opens automatically when toilet used

floor joists

airtight cover opens automatically when bin lid opened

air vent

cover can be lifted to add garden rubbish

cellar

wastes from toilet and kitchen

soil and leaf mould mix

air vents

air intake

Down the drain

The material you flush into the sewers contains a mixture of different chemicals in water. The amount of liquid that passes along a sewer every day is called the flow.

Sewage contains natural pollutants that can encourage the growth of bacteria. These bacteria use up the oxygen dissolved in rivers. This can mean there is none left for fish and other water animals. The biological oxygen demand (BOD) is a measure of how much oxygen these bacteria would use up to grow. The BOD of sewage must be reduced before it is released into a river.

Ammonia is a poisonous chemical that goes into the sewers. It is an alkaline gas and can kill many types of river life.

In areas where there are lots of metal works, sewage can also contain small amounts of metals like cadmium and lead. These are very poisonous and must be removed.

There are lots of other bits and pieces in sewage: scraps of paper, grit and stones, even metal bars and bricks.

Choosing a site for a sewage works

Measling is a typical Midlands town. It is on the route of a new motorway, and the local council expect this will bring new development to the area. A large industrial estate is already planned next to the new road. Over 500 new houses will be built on the other side of the town.

The old sewage works was built in the 1930s and is now in a bad state of repair. It will not cope with the increased demand. The local water company has to build a new works.

● How big does the new works need to be? Use the information on the printed sheets to design and cost a suitable sewage works.

● Where should the new works be built? Three possible sites are shown on the map: A, B and C. Prepare a report listing the advantages and disadvantages of each site.

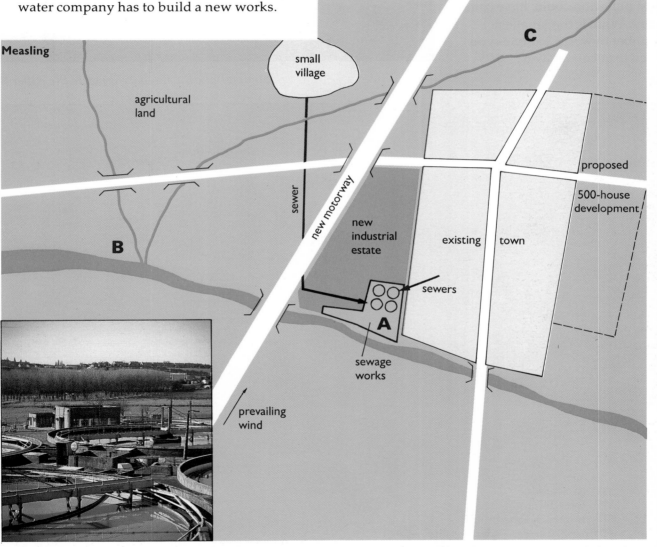

EXTRAS

1 Sewage is only one part of the rubbish we throw away. Keep a record of the stuff your family puts in the dustbin every week. Prepare a plan to deal with it most efficiently. You could consider recycling, burning, burying in the ground or dumping at sea.

2 Find out where your local sewage works is. Where does it discharge the waste?

17·8 Dirty water

The map shows an area just north of Durham. Lumley Park Burn is a small river flowing into the River Wear. Samples of water were taken from where the burn enters the Wear. Imagine that one day the samples were unusually acidic.

● Using the samples of water provided, work out where the acid pollution could have come from. What is the smallest number of water samples you need to get an answer?

Lumley Park Burn where it meets the River Wear

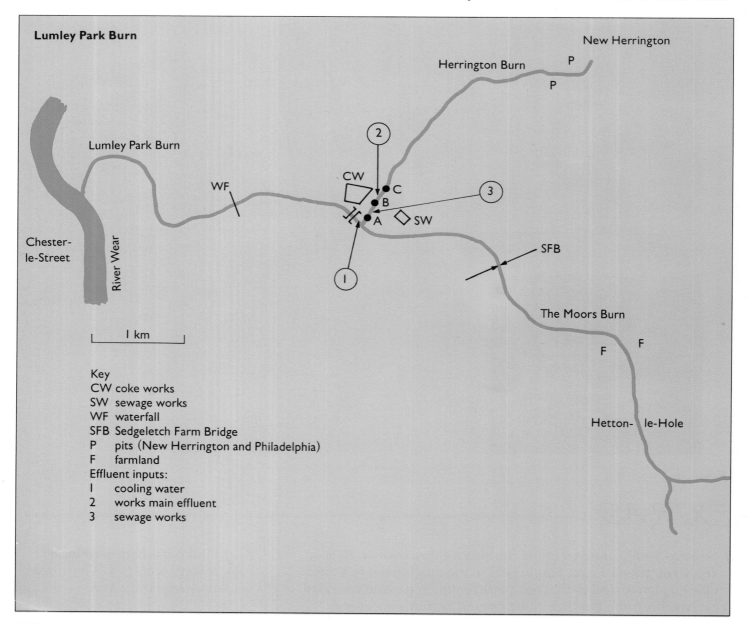

Key
CW coke works
SW sewage works
WF waterfall
SFB Sedgeletch Farm Bridge
P   pits (New Herrington and Philadelphia)
F   farmland
Effluent inputs:
1   cooling water
2   works main effluent
3   sewage works

Accidents

Pollution accidents often have devastating effects on an area. In November 1986, a fire broke out at a warehouse near Basel in Switzerland. In the warehouse were nearly 1000 tonnes of pesticides and about 12 tonnes of compounds containing mercury. Water that was used to fight the fire then drained into the Rhine. It carried some of these poisons. Biologists could still detect the poison when the Rhine reached the North Sea 600 km further on.

The Rhine – pollution 'sans frontières'

Communicating

A river study

Most of the pollution that ends up in our rivers is not accidental. Factories, sewage works and farmers are allowed to discharge a certain amount of waste into rivers without breaking the law. What effect does this have?

Tests on water samples from Lumley Park Burn

	Nitrate (mg/l)	Ammonia (mg/l)	Phosphate (mg/l)	Oxygen (%)
Lumley Park Burn	35	2.5	3	100
Site A	0	12.5	5	50
Site B	0	10	0	70
Site C	0	0.5	0	80
Sedgeletch Farm Bridge	50	0	0.5	70

1 Where is the highest oxygen concentration recorded?

2 Which part of the burn has the most nitrate pollution?

3 Where do you think the nitrate is coming from?

4 Where do you think the phosphate is coming from?

5 The oxygen content is very high just below the waterfall. Why?

6 The level of ammonia in Lumley Park Burn is lower than in Herrington Burn. Why?

● Use information from this page to prepare a report for the local paper. It should describe the pollution in Lumley Park Burn. You should also give details of the long-term problems for rivers in this area.

EXTRAS

1 Some companies deliberately break the laws about discharging waste into lakes and rivers. Why do you think they do this? Write your own law to protect lakes and rivers from pollution. How could you make sure it is obeyed? What punishment would you give for breaking your law?

2 Design a kit to take out with you to rivers. It should have equipment for taking important measures of pollution. What would you include? And why?

3 How much water does your family use every week? Work out a way of finding out and then try it. Use your water bill to estimate how much you pay per litre of water.

17·9 Cars and roads

Most of the lead added to petrol comes out in the vehicle's exhaust. This makes a fine lead dust that settles very close to the road.

1 Why is this dangerous?

How much risk are you taking? ⚠ 📄

Plot the levels of lead in the dust in your area.
Each group in your class should cover a different site.
Try to find out if there are any areas of high lead concentration and work out what is causing them. Plot your results on a map of your neighbourhood.

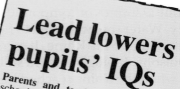

Lead lowers pupils' IQs

Parents and teachers today called for all schools near motorways to be relocated.

The leaked results of a national survey show that pupils who live and attend primary schools near Britain's motorways scored below average marks in standard tests.

This is bound to increase concern in the wake of last week's admission that car exhausts pump 3000 tonnes of lead into Britain's air every year.

A spokesperson for the DES said 'We will study the report carefully when it is published. This is a very complicated question and more research may be needed.' She concluded 'The DES is not responsible for choosing the sites of schools. That is a matter for the local authority.'

Nobody in the Minister of Transport's office was available to comment.

'This is a disgraceful situation.' said Mr

Kestrels flourish on the wildlife of motorway verges

People and cars do not mix well

The petrol engine

A car engine needs petrol and oxygen (from air) to work properly. When the petrol burns, it expands and pushes against a piston. Most cars have at least four pistons and cylinders to keep the wheels going smoothly.

Petrol is a mixture. It contains about 400 different hydrocarbons and small amounts of other chemicals. A hydrocarbon is a compound containing only the elements carbon and hydrogen. When these burn they combine with oxygen to make water and carbon dioxide. Unfortunately the engine does not always get enough oxygen and the poisonous gas, carbon monoxide, can be formed.

Air contains nitrogen as well as oxygen. These react in the heat and pressure of the engine to produce nitrogen oxides. Nitrogen oxides are harmful, acid gases.

Some petrol also has lead added to it. This helps to smooth the engine's running. Unfortunately, it is also a health hazard.

Making cars cleaner

The lean-burn engine

This type of engine mixes a much larger amount of air with its petrol to make sure no carbon monoxide is produced. It also gives more miles to the gallon than older engine types.

Lead-free petrol

At first unleaded petrol was more expensive than leaded petrol. Motorists were not certain about whether their cars could use unleaded petrol. Many cars needed a small adjustment to the engine. Some people said that cars lost performance when using unleaded petrol. Even garages were not always sure. The situation now is clearer in the UK. All cars made since October 1990 must be able to run on unleaded petrol.

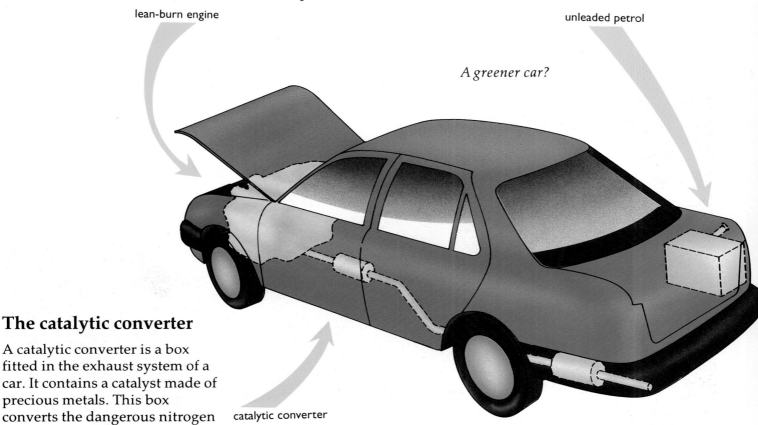

lean-burn engine

unleaded petrol

A greener car?

catalytic converter

The catalytic converter

A catalytic converter is a box fitted in the exhaust system of a car. It contains a catalyst made of precious metals. This box converts the dangerous nitrogen oxides back into harmless nitrogen gas. It also changes carbon monoxide to carbon dioxide. Any unburned hydrocarbons from the engine are also converted to carbon dioxide and water.

- Give two reasons why motorists were slow to use unleaded petrol at first.
- Write down two things that encouraged motorists to switch to unleaded petrol.
- Make up a leaflet about the catalytic converter.

EXTRAS

1 How did you get to school this morning? By car? Train? Bicycle? Walking? Make a list of the advantages and disadvantages of each method of transport.

2 Design the perfect 'green car'. Would it be driven by petrol or electricity? Would it be large or small? Would it use metals or plastics for its body? Give reasons for all the decisions you make. List all the ways that your 'green' car affects the environment.

3 How many of the cars in the school car park can use unleaded petrol? Do a survey to find out how many do.

Living in cities

Eight out of ten people in Britain live in cities. How good is their environment? How does it compare with living in the country?

Observing

- Make a list of all the good and bad points about city life. Are the things that are good about living in a city bad in the country?
- Use your lists to help design a scoring system for environments. It should give points for every good thing about an environment and take points away for bad things.
  - Take someone else's system and try it out on your way home from school.
  - Is everyone's system the same?

Measuring environmental quality

Different people have different ideas about what is important. How can you 'measure' the environment? Here are some ideas you could try.

Noise

How much noise is there in your area?

1 Where do the most annoying noises come from?
2 Design a scale for assessing how 'bad' a noise is.

Traffic

Cars are an important part of city life. But do they help or spoil the environment?

3 How many cars and lorries pass along your street every day?
4 Which parts of your town or city have most traffic?
5 Are there any parts where cars are not allowed?
6 Can you find a link between the number of vehicles in a road and the level of dust? Or the noise?

Dust

You can use a piece of Sellotape to check for dust.

7 Do things get dustier near roads?
8 How can you produce a figure for dustiness from your investigations?

Litter

Everyone can see the difference between somewhere with lots of litter and somewhere with very little.

9 How can you produce a figure for the amount of litter in an area?

10 Where does most of the litter come from?

Graffiti

Some people think all graffiti is vandalism.

11 How much graffiti can you find? Is it all bad?

12 What other types of vandalism can you find?

13 Which areas suffer from the most damage?

Parks

Most people like green parks. But how much parkland do we need? Use maps of your area to see how much space is given to parks and gardens.

14 How does your area compare with others?

15 What is most of the space used for?

Communicating

Displaying your findings

Working as a class you should be able to gather a large amount of information about your local environment.

● Prepare an exhibition (maybe for your school hall or a local library) to display your findings.

16 What features would visitors like to see?

17 What would you like to see improved?

Difficult choices

The needs of the city often lead to major threats to the countryside. Large areas may be needed for houses, water supplies, factories, mining, roads or airports.

Developments like these involve difficult choices. There are many reasons both for and against going ahead. How do we decide?

● Use the worksheet to look at the choices that must be made in deciding about an opencast coal mine.

EXTRAS

1 Imagine you are a local councillor. What laws would you pass for your area? Pick three bye-laws that you think would have the best effect and explain why.

2 Think about your school environment. Pick one small area that needs improving.

● What is wrong with it?

● How can the situation be improved?

3 If you used your scoring system on a city environment, use it to mark a place in the country. If you used it on the country, mark the city. Does your system work just as well for both? You probably prefer the environment which has the better score. How can you design a 'fair' system that doesn't depend so much on your own views?

The future?

Docklands school closes

The Saint Hilda Comprehensive in Old London's Docklands area closed today for the last time. Rising sea levels have caused regular flooding into the ground floor of the building. The local council have decided it would be cheaper to build a completely new school on higher ground than try to keep water out of Saint Hilda's.

LATE NEWS

2000 Danes homeless

The storms which battered western Europe yesterday combined with spring tides to breach Denmark's coastal defences. Much of the city of Esbjerg is now under water.

Canadian drought continues

A FURTHER DEVALUATION of the Canadian dollar is expected today. This follows the anouncement earlier this week of another record-breaking fall in Canadian wheat production.

Prime Minister Gilbert Lecroix is quoted as saying, 'The country's economy is on its last legs. The change in rainfall patterns has destroyed our farms.'

Meanwhile the price of shares in Superwheat the largest grain producing company in the world rose sharply. The fall in supply will almost certainly mean higher profits for the multinational company. Superwheat owns large areas of land in the fertile wheat belt of North Africa.

- Discuss how each news item might be linked to global warming.

- Using information from the following page, try to invent some headlines of your own. How might global warming affect your own school?

- Prepare your own newspaper article. It should show what might happen in your area over the fifty years from 1990 to 2040. Remember that things that happen a long way away can have an effect on you. If the weather changes and crops fail, where will you get your food?

Carbon dioxide and the rainforests

Carbon dioxide is essential to life. Plants take it in through their leaves and use it to make food. They give out oxygen as a waste gas. The process is photosynthesis. It keeps the carbon dioxide level in the air down and the oxygen level up.

Tiny plants floating in the oceans and equatorial rainforests are huge stores of very active plants.

The carbon cycle

Carbon is a very important element. It is recycled through living things. Plants and animals break down food to give them energy and help them to grow. This process uses up oxygen and gives off carbon dioxide. It is called respiration.

1 What has happened to the temperature of the world over the last 100 years?

2 What do you think is likely to happen to the temperature over the next 100 years?

3 Can you think of any problems this might cause?

4 What other changes in the weather do you predict for the next 100 years?

5 Can you find any evidence to support the idea that pollution is causing the changes?

6 How are green plants helping to keep the Earth cool?

7 Draw a flow diagram to show the cycling of carbon through photosynthesis and respiration.

8 What would happen if photosynthesis worked much faster than respiration as the temperature got hotter?

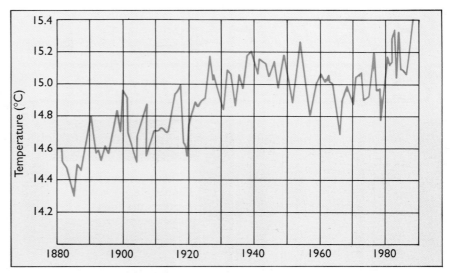

Average world temperature since 1880

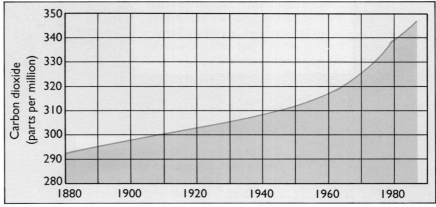

Average concentration of carbon dioxide in the atmosphere since 1880

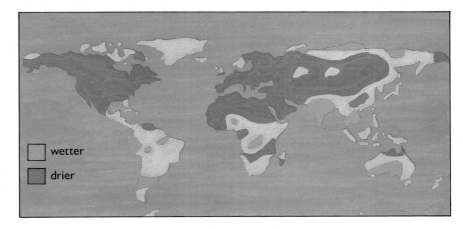

One prediction of how climate may change: yellow areas will stay about the same

EXTRAS

1 One way to cut down carbon dioxide production is to burn less fossil fuels. What are fossil fuels? How can we use less of them?

2 Imagine this is an extract from *Television Times* in 2040. Can you explain what changed to stop the Earth warming up?

8.15 Great scientific hoaxes 13: The greenhouse effect
Barely 50 years ago newspapers were full of reports of the impending doom for the human race. What caused this panic? Watch Channel 309 at 8.15 for the final episode in Dr Phibes's documentary series on scientific hoaxes of the last century.

18 BODIES
18·1 Bones and muscles

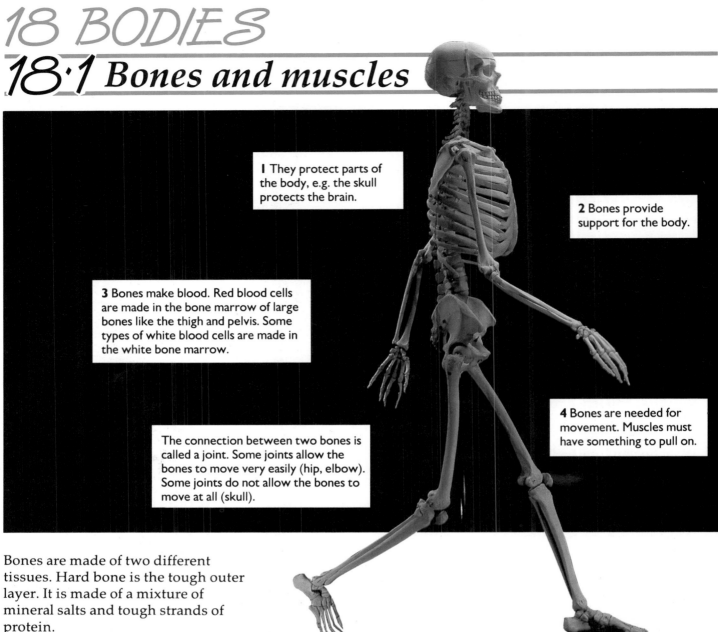

1 They protect parts of the body, e.g. the skull protects the brain.

2 Bones provide support for the body.

3 Bones make blood. Red blood cells are made in the bone marrow of large bones like the thigh and pelvis. Some types of white blood cells are made in the white bone marrow.

The connection between two bones is called a joint. Some joints allow the bones to move very easily (hip, elbow). Some joints do not allow the bones to move at all (skull).

4 Bones are needed for movement. Muscles must have something to pull on.

Bones are made of two different tissues. Hard bone is the tough outer layer. It is made of a mixture of mineral salts and tough strands of protein.

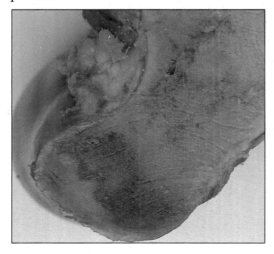

Bones are hollow. The marrow inside the bone is soft. It helps to make blood and keeps the hard bone alive.

Broken bones

Bones are living things. They can usually repair themselves if they are broken. The doctor uses bandages or splints to keep the broken ends in the right position.

Some older people suffer with *brittle bones*. The bones become weak and break very easily. The problem is much more common in women than men. Doctors are still trying to find out what causes this problem.

Investigating

How strong are bones? ⚠️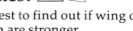
● Design and carry out a test to find out if wing or leg bones from a chicken are stronger.

Muscles

The human body has about 650 muscles. They make up about 40% of the total body weight.

Muscles are made of protein. They are able to change chemical energy in sugar into movement energy. When this happens, only 25% of the sugar energy is changed into movement. Three-quarters of it is wasted as heat. This is why you get hot and sweat when you exercise.

food

one-quarter of energy used in movement

three-quarters of energy wasted in movement

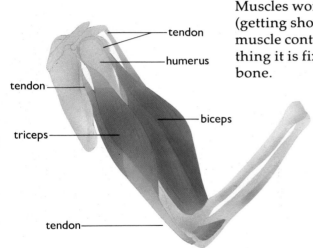

tendon

humerus

tendon

triceps

biceps

tendon

Muscles work by contracting (getting shorter). When the muscle contracts, it pulls the thing it is fixed to, usually a bone.

Muscles cannot push so they have to work in pairs. One muscle pulls one way and the other pulls in the opposite direction. These pairs are called *antagonistic muscles*. The biceps raises your arm and the triceps straightens it.

The connections between muscles and bones are called *tendons*. If a tendon is cut, the bone cannot be controlled.

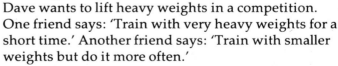

Planning

Lifting weights

Dave wants to lift heavy weights in a competition. One friend says: 'Train with very heavy weights for a short time.' Another friend says: 'Train with smaller weights but do it more often.'

● Plan an investigation to find out which is better.

EXTRAS

1 Who has the strongest muscles? Design and carry out a fair test for one muscle (e.g. biceps). Are people with thicker muscles stronger?

2 Build a model finger. It should have three sections like a real one, and be joined to an artificial hand. How many muscles do you need to make the finger move like a real one? You can use lengths of string or elastic for the muscles. Feel your arm to find where the muscles that move your fingers are.

18·2 Heart and lungs

Heart rate 60 beats per minute
Breathing rate 10 litres per minute

Heart rate 170 beats per minute
Breathing rate 140 litres per minute

Heart rate 140 beats per minute.
Breathing rate 100 litres per minute

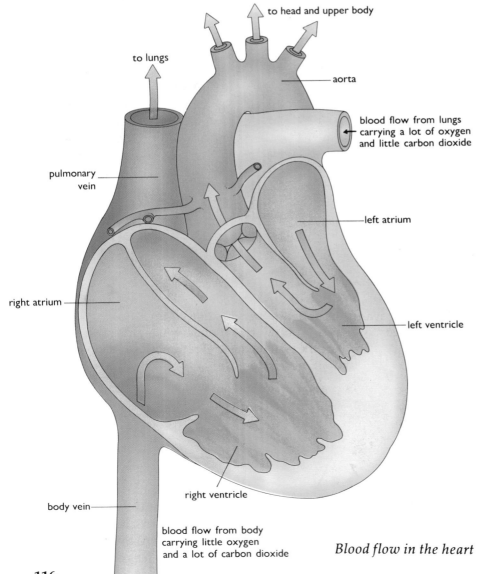

to head and upper body

to lungs

aorta

blood flow from lungs carrying a lot of oxygen and little carbon dioxide

pulmonary vein

left atrium

right atrium

left ventricle

right ventricle

body vein

blood flow from body carrying little oxygen and a lot of carbon dioxide

Blood flow in the heart

The heart-lung system

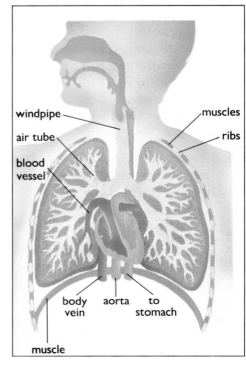

windpipe

air tube

blood vessel

muscles

ribs

body vein

aorta

to stomach

muscle

Breathing

The lungs have to get oxygen into the body and carbon dioxide out of it. They work by getting air and blood close together. In the lungs, oxygen passes from the air into the blood. The oxygen dissolves in blood and is carried round the body. The carbon dioxide made by the body passes into the blood. When the blood gets to the lungs, the carbon dioxide passes into the air that is breathed out. This stale air can then be pushed out by the chest muscles.

The lungs have a very thin layer of cells which keeps the blood and air separate.

What happens inside an alveolus

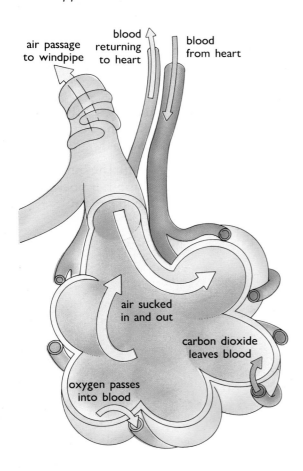

Respiration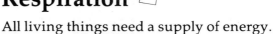

All living things need a supply of energy. Animals get this supply from food.

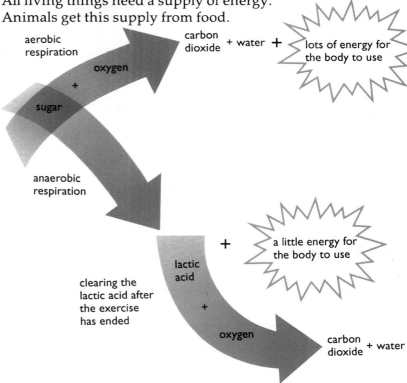

Respiration turns energy in food into energy that the body can use. It happens in every living cell in the body. Usually, the cells use oxygen from the blood to release energy from food. This is *aerobic* respiration. Sometimes the body needs energy so fast that it cannot get enough oxygen from the blood. *Anaerobic* respiration can give a boost of extra energy if aerobic respiration is working as fast as it can. It leaves waste, like lactic acid, in the body.

1 How does the oxygen needed for aerobic respiration get to the cells in the foot?
2 How does the carbon dioxide made by aerobic respiration leave the human body?
3 How does the food needed for respiration reach all the cells of the body?
4 Explain why the heart rate and breathing rate change for the runner shown on the opposite page.
5 It takes a while for the heart rate and breathing rate to fall after the runner has finished. Why?

EXTRAS

1 A commentator at the Olympic Games described a runner as 'swimming in a sea of lactic acid'.
(**a**) What did she mean?
(**b**) What effect would it have on the runner?
(**c**) Would a 10 000 metre runner have the same problem? Explain.

Investigating
2 Some people with breathing problems cannot blow air out of their lungs very well. Design and make a device that can measure how hard someone can 'puff'. Use it to find out who can breathe out the strongest. Think about hygiene.

Blood

Adult human beings have about 5 litres of blood (more than enough to fill a large bucket). A new born baby has about 300 ml or a mug full.

The contents of a litre of blood

plasma
 – mainly water, but also contains
 – salts
 – sugar
 – fat droplets
 – proteins (for clotting and defence against disease)
 – urea and other wastes

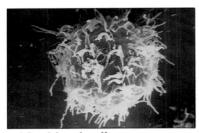

white blood cells
 – protect the body against disease

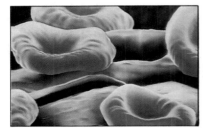

red blood cells
 – carry oxygen round the body

platelets
 – very small particles that help the blood to clot

Blood normally flows round the body in tubes. If it leaks out, it can cause a bruise. The bruising is caused by the red blood cells breaking down.

Arteries, capillaries and veins

Arteries are thick-walled tubes which carry blood from the heart. They must have thick walls to stand up to the pressure of the blood.

Capillaries are very thin tubes running through every tissue in the body. No cell is more than 1 millimetre away from a capillary. Many cells are much closer. Oxygen and food pass from the blood to the cells. Wastes like carbon dioxide pass into the blood.

Capillaries join to make larger tubes called veins. These carry blood back to the heart. The heart then passes the blood to the lungs.

After the blood has gone through the lungs, it goes back to the heart. It gets another push and begins its journey round the body again.

Haemoglobin

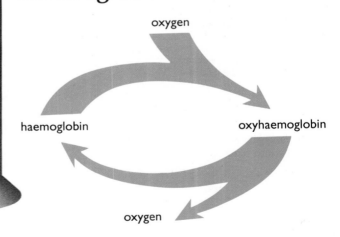

The haemoglobin cycle

Haemoglobin is a chemical in red blood cells. It takes up oxygen when there is a lot of oxygen present. This happens in the lungs. The haemoglobin is converted to *oxyhaemoglobin*.

Cells use up oxygen in respiration. This reduces the level of oxygen and the oxyhaemoglobin breaks down to give oxygen to the cells.

1 Which part of the blood carries oxygen round the body?

2 Where is food loaded into the blood?

3 How much of the blood is made of red cells?

4 What parts of the blood are used to make a scab?

5 Anaemia is an illness in which the red blood cells do not work properly. How will this affect the body?

6 When someone is ill, the number of white blood cells goes up. Why is this useful to the body?

The gut

Many parts of the gut wall have special cells which produce *enzymes*. These enzymes help to break down the large food molecules into smaller ones.

Glands in the stomach lining. These give out digestive juices

The gut has two jobs:
- breaking down food so that it can be absorbed into the body,
- helping the food molecules into the blood so that they can be carried round the body

Both jobs are done as the food passes along the gut.

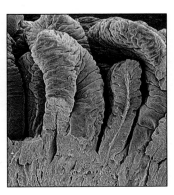

Scanning electron micrograph of villi showing the large surface area

The surface of the small intestine is covered with finger shapes called *villi*. The villi give the gut a very large surface area. This gives food molecules more chance to pass into the blood.

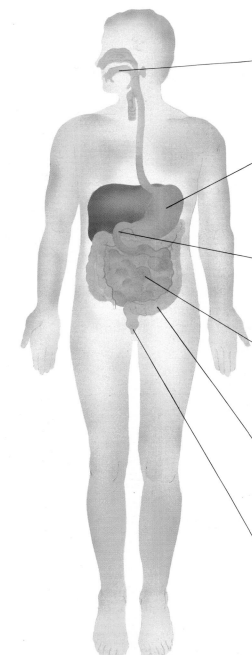

The digestive system

Mouth
Teeth break down large lumps of food into smaller particles.
Enzymes in saliva break large starch molecules into smaller sugar molecules.

Stomach
Acid in stomach kills germs and helps to break down protein-rich foods.
Enzyme pepsin breaks large protein molecues.

Duodenum
Bile from liver helps to neutralise acid from stomach.
Enzymes from pancreas break down proteins, starches and fats.

Small intestine
Digestion continues. Most large molecules are converted to small molecules. These can pass through the gut wall into the blood.

Large intestine
Digestion complete. Water absorbed to make wastes more solid.
Some bacteria living here make vitamins which can be absorbed.

Rectum
Wastes stored until they can be passed out of the body.

Communicating

Have you got the guts?

- You have been given the job of explaining how the gut works for a TV science programme. You have a ten-minute slot in the programme which will be broadcast at 7.30 in the evening. Many children and adults will be watching. The producer wants you to include at least one working model, an experiment and a chart.

- You must also prepare a factsheet. This will be given free to anyone who writes in. It will be printed in two colours on both sides of an A4 sheet of paper.

18·4 *Eyes and ears*

In a normal eye, the *lens* and *cornea* focus a sharp image on the *retina*.

Long sight

Sometimes the lens and cornea are not strong enough to bend the light into focus on the retina. The image is focussed behind the retina. The person suffers from long sight. He or she cannot see objects close to their eyes clearly, but can focus on distant things. Long sight can be corrected with a convex lens.

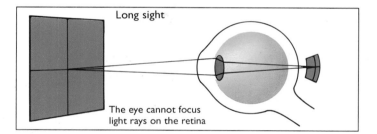

Long sight

The eye cannot focus light rays on the retina

Short sight

Sometimes the cornea and lens are too strong. They focus the image in front of the retina. This person suffers from short sight. He or she cannot see distant objects clearly, but can focus on things near their eyes. This can be corrected with a concave lens.

▼ *Correcting long sight*

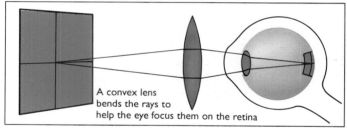

A convex lens bends the rays to help the eye focus them on the retina

Astigmatism

Astigmatism occurs if the cornea and lens of the eye are not a regular shape. The person cannot focus on different parts of the view at the same time. This can be corrected with a special lens.

Investigating

An eye test

- Design eye tests for long and short sightedness. They should work with small children who cannot read. They will not know letters of the alphabet.
- Try your tests on your class.

1 Do they give the same results as a normal eye test?

Hearing

Sound is a pattern of wave movements in the air.

1 The waves push against the ear drum and make it move in and out.
2 The pattern of movements passes along the bones of the middle ear. They magnify the force of the wave movement and pass it into liquid in the cochlea.
3 The cochlea is full of liquid. The liquid is harder to move than air. This is why the bones magnify the force of the original wave pattern.
4 Special cells in the cochlea move with the liquid waves. This is a bit like the way strands of seaweed move when a wave passes over them.
5 The special cells send nerve impulses to the brain. The brain decodes the signals and we hear them as sounds.

The human ear can just detect a sound 1000 times quieter than a whisper. Many animals are even more sensitive to sound. Ears also have the job of keeping the body balanced. We know which way is up because of sense cells in the inner ear.

A small child wearing a hearing aid

Hearing problems

Some hearing aids work by amplifying sound before it enters the ear. Problems with the ear drum or ear bones can usually be helped by hearing aids. If the inner ear or nerve is damaged, hearing aids are not very helpful.

Glue ear occurs when mucus builds up inside the middle ear. The mucus tends to dampen the movement of the ear bones. The usual treatment is a medicine to clear out the mucus. In the worst cases little tubes called *grommets* are put through the ear drum. These drain away the mucus .

Ear ache is common in children. It can be very painful but is usually cured fairly quickly by antibiotics. These drugs kill the bacteria that are causing the infection.

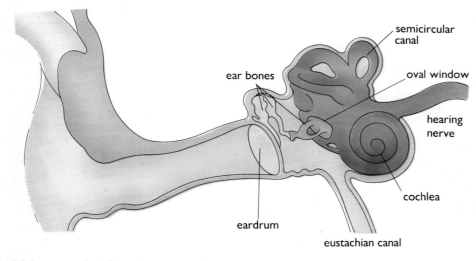

semicircular canal

oval window

ear bones

hearing nerve

cochlea

eardrum

eustachian canal

Older people's hearing sometimes gets worse. This may be due to the joints between the bones of the middle ear getting stiff. They cannot move as easily as those in younger people. The vibrations do not pass so well. There is no cure for this except for other people to speak more loudly and be patient!

EXTRAS

1 Ear trumpets were the first hearing aids. A trumpet is like a large funnel which directs sounds into the ear. Try to make an ear trumpet. Which works better: a long, thin trumpet or a short wide one?

2 Films in other languages often have subtitles in English when they are shown on British television. Find out the best way to show these subtitles on the the screen.
(a) Should they be white on a black background, black writing against the normal picture or some other system?
(b) Where should they be on the screen?
(c) How many words can people read at one go?
Use some photographs from a magazine and some cut out typed messages to find out (or see if you can do it with a computer and video recorder).

Studs Malone

The rain came on suddenly. A flash of lightning and, a second later, a rumble of thunder. Studs had just time to turn up his coat collar before the first drops splattered onto his face. He swore softly under his breath.

The dame was trouble, he knew that, but she was... well, kind of cute. And he'd always had a soft spot for a damsel in distress. He wondered if he was a fool for taking the case.

A car pulled up beside him. He felt suspicious. Something was wrong.

The barrel of a shotgun appeared out of a back window. He threw himself to the floor just in time to hear the shot go over his head. People around screamed and ran for cover. He reached for his own gun and rolled over behind a lamp post. Somehow, it was comforting to feel the solid metal between him and his attackers. The gun fired again. More screams and this time a hot dog joint behind him got some extra air conditioning.

He managed to get in one shot. He must have been lucky. The car burst into a ball of flame and black smoke joined the smell of hot dogs on the evening air.

It was five minutes before the fat policeman ran up, blowing his whistle. Studs was already warming himself by the wreck of the car. The rain had stopped and his coat was beginning to dry. Studs grunted, 'Every cloud has a silver lining.'

'Mr Malone...' It was the dame, all breathless. She had been running. 'I've got to warn you – you're in terrible danger! You must leave town now!'

'Yeh.' Studs grimaced at the acid taste of burnt rubber in his mouth. 'Now tell me the real reason the mob are after me, babe. And why do I get this feeling you're bad news?'

A *stimulus* is something that Studs notices. It might be a smell, a sound, a taste or a flash of light.
A *detector* is the sense organ Studs uses to detect the stimulus. His eye is the detector for a flash of light.
The *response* is what Studs will do. Maybe it is running away, or frowning.
An *effector* is the part of her body that lets Studs do this. Muscles are the most common effectors in humans.

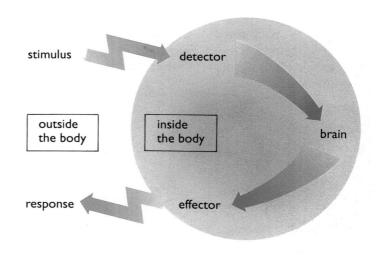

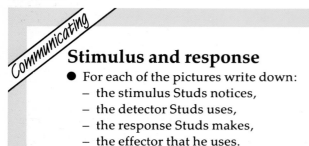

Stimulus and response

● For each of the pictures write down:
  - the stimulus Studs notices,
  - the detector Studs uses,
  - the response Studs makes,
  - the effector that he uses.

All our responses are controlled by a system of nerves. The brain and spinal cord are called the central nervous system. Other nerves stretch throughout the body. They take messages to and from the central nervous system.

The brain contains about 14 million million cells and has a mass of about 1.5 kilograms. It looks a bit like a greyish-pink jelly.

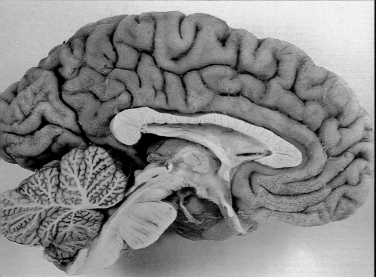
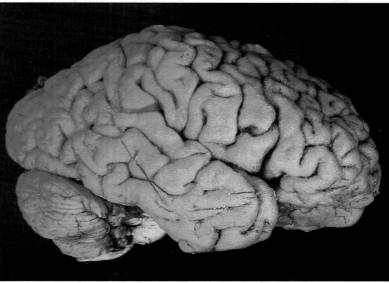

A human brain

EXTRAS

1 Sometimes the brain can be confused. Optical illusions are difficult for the brain to interpret. Look at some illusions.

(a) Can you explain why the brain is confused?
(b) Try to make some illusions of your own.

2 The table shows the sizes of animals' bodies and brains.
(a) Do bigger animals have bigger brains?
(b) Do cleverer animals have bigger brains?
Find a good way to display the information and your answers.

Mass	Human	Chimpanzee	Elephant	Blue whale
body (kg)	70	50	5550	90 800
brain (kg)	1.5	0.6	5.4	5.2

When humans are born, males and females look very similar. As they grow, changes begin to appear. The changes become obvious at puberty when children become adults.

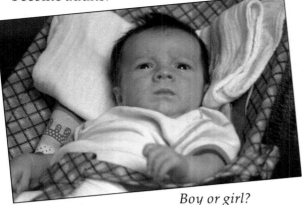

Boy or girl?

Males

At puberty the pituitary gland, near the base of the brain, starts to release a chemical into the blood. This switches on the testes. They start to produce sperm and release other chemicals that cause a number of growth changes. In the male these lead to:
– growth of body and facial hair,
– a deeper voice,
– the penis and testes growing bigger,
– the body becoming bigger and more
  muscular.

The chemicals released into the blood are called *hormones*. All these growth changes are controlled by hormones. Some are produced by the brain and some are produced by the testes.

In some cultures these changes are marked by special ceremonies which mark the change from a boy to a man.

Growing pains

The rise in hormone levels can have other effects and not all of them are easy to understand.

The skin can become greasier. *Acne* is more common in teenagers than other people. Boys suffer from acne more than girls. The only cure is plenty of soap and water until the hormones settle down again.

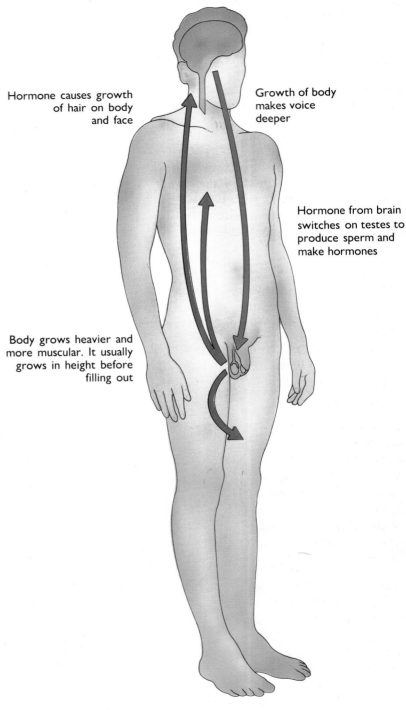

Hormone causes growth of hair on body and face

Growth of body makes voice deeper

Hormone from brain switches on testes to produce sperm and make hormones

Body grows heavier and more muscular. It usually grows in height before filling out

The body gets taller very quickly. There are many teenage boys who are thin and gangly. The body takes longer to grow in width. Males may not reach their full adult size until their early twenties. Females become physically mature in their late teens.

Puberty can be a very confusing time. However, growing problems are usually only temporary. By the age of twenty they have usually disappeared.

Females

The female reproductive system is more complicated than the male. It has two jobs:
- to produce eggs,
- to protect any fertilised eggs until birth.

Females also produce milk to feed the growing baby after birth. All these different jobs are controlled by hormones.

At puberty, a special gland near the base of the brain starts to release a hormone. This switches on the ovaries. They start to produce hormones that produce a number of growth changes. In the female these make:
- the breasts grow bigger,
- the uterus and ovaries develop,
- the ovaries start to release eggs,
- the body hair grow,
- the shape of the body become more rounded.

The ovaries have a store of eggs; one of these is usually released every month. The timing depends on a complicated pattern of hormones. These make sure the uterus is ready to support the growing baby if the egg is fertilised.

If the egg is fertilised, hormones also stop any more eggs being released until the pregnancy is over. If the egg is not fertilised, the wall of the uterus breaks down. It is released from the body with some blood. This is *menstruation* (or a monthly period). The next time an egg is released the uterus wall builds up again.

This pattern repeats itself until the *menopause*. At the menopause, the pattern of hormones changes. No more eggs are released from the ovaries and a woman cannot have any more children.

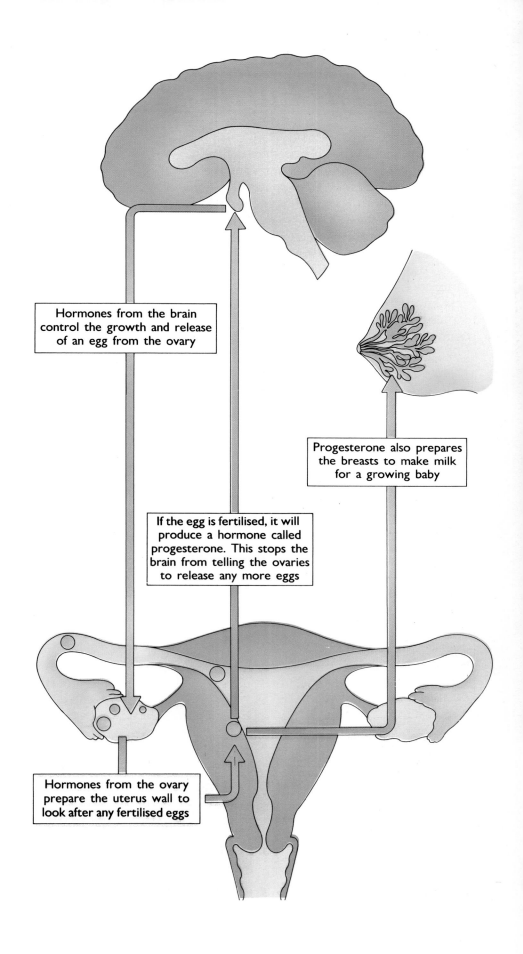

Hormones from the brain control the growth and release of an egg from the ovary

Progesterone also prepares the breasts to make milk for a growing baby

If the egg is fertilised, it will produce a hormone called progesterone. This stops the brain from telling the ovaries to release any more eggs

Hormones from the ovary prepare the uterus wall to look after any fertilised eggs

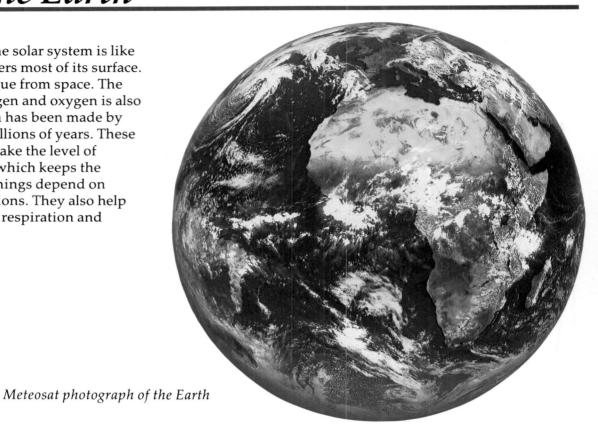

19 SPACE
19·1 The Earth

No other planet in the solar system is like the Earth. Water covers most of its surface. This makes it look blue from space. The atmosphere of nitrogen and oxygen is also unusual. The oxygen has been made by green plants over millions of years. These plants also help to make the level of carbon dioxide low which keeps the planet cool. Living things depend on these strange conditions. They also help to maintain them by respiration and photosynthesis.

Meteosat photograph of the Earth

City	Latitude	Angle of Sun on 21 June	Hours of daylight on 21 June	Average temperature on 21 June	Angle of Sun on 21 December	Hours of daylight on 21 December	Average temperature on 21 December	Main vegetation type
Reykjavik, Iceland	64°10′ N	49°20′	23	8°C	2°20′	4	3°C	tundra and ice desert
Glasgow, Scotland	53°30′ N	57°38′	18	18°C	10°41′	7	5°C	broad-leaved forest
Montreal, Canada	45°42′ N	67°48′	16	11°C	20°48′	8	−5°C	coniferous forest
Lagos, Nigeria	6°20′ N	72°14′	11	28°C	60°10′	11	28°C	rainforest
Singapore, S.E. Asia	1°00′ N	67°30′	10	27°C	65°30′	11	24°C	rainforest
Perth, Australia	32°00′ S	34°30′	9	12°C	81°30′	13	21°C	evergreen forest
Buenos Aires, Argentina	34°50′ S	31°40′	8	10°C	79°00′	14	22°C	grassland

Energy from the Sun

All life on Earth depends on energy from the Sun. Three things affect the amount of energy that any place on the Earth gets:
- where the place is,
- the time of day,
- the season of the year.

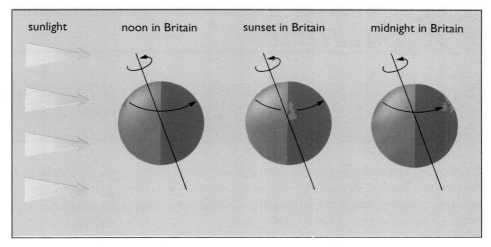

Day and night

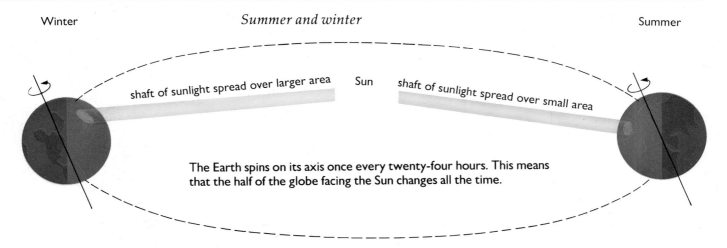

Winter   *Summer and winter*   Summer

shaft of sunlight spread over larger area   Sun   shaft of sunlight spread over small area

The Earth spins on its axis once every twenty-four hours. This means that the half of the globe facing the Sun changes all the time.

The seasons are a result of the Earth's tilt. Because of the Earth's tilt, different parts of it face the Sun during a year. This has two effects:
- the height of the Sun in the sky at midday changes,
- the length of the day changes.

In summer, sunlight is spread over a small area of the Earth. The Sun is high in the sky and the shadows are short. The ground heats up more quickly as more sunlight energy is concentrated on a small area.

1. What is the average temperature in Reykjavik on 21 December?
2. Which cities have the biggest range of temperatures throughout the year?
3. Which cities have temperatures below 15 °C in the summer?
4. 'The average temperature is controlled by the latitude of the city.'
   - Give some evidence from the table that supports this idea.
   - Give some evidence from the table that does not support this idea.
5. What connection is there between the latitude of a city and the length of the day on 21 June?
6. Stonehenge is a site that is linked to Sun worship. How high would the Sun be in the sky on Midsummer's Day, 21 June? The latitude of Stonehenge is 51° 10′N.

EXTRAS

1. Design and make a device to measure the angle of the Sun in the sky. You must never look directly at the Sun!

2. Some modern buildings use the change in the height of the Sun in the sky. They have windows which allow the weak winter sunlight in but keep the hot summer Sun out. This means the building heats up in winter but stays cooler in summer. Think of some way to design this type of building.

19·2 Satellites

Satellites circle the Earth above the atmosphere. The smallest satellites are the remains of spacecraft sent up years ago. Some of these mini-satellites could be a screw or a nut from one of these craft. Most satellites are more useful than this. They are used for weather reports, television and radio communications and scientific research. The path a satellite takes around the Earth is called its orbit.

1 What is the Earth's largest satellite?

The first satellite was launched by the Russians in 1957. It was called Sputnik 1 and had a mass of 84 kg, roughly the same as a large adult. The rocket that lifted this into orbit had a mass of 500 tonnes.

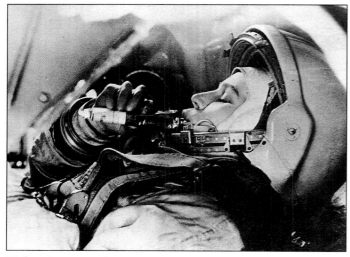

Valentina Tereshkova

Sputnik fell back to Earth after 92 days. It passed through the top of the atmosphere once during every orbit. Air friction slowed it down so that, each time round, it flew slower and lower. Eventually the small spacecraft fell towards Earth although it never reached the surface. It burned up on the way down because of friction with the atmosphere.

Valentina Tereshkova was the first woman in space. She was the pilot of Vostok 6 which was launched on 16 June 1963. Valentina had volunteered to train as a cosmonaut after Yuri Gagarin's flight in 1961. Unlike most of the male cosmonauts, she was not a trained jet pilot. She was a worker in a textile mill who had taken up parachuting as a hobby.

American rumours said that she did not enjoy the flight but she was not allowed down until she had completed forty eight orbits. The Soviet premier, Krushchev, was keen to win another 'first' over the Americans in the space race. Officially, the mission was a great success.

● Imagine that you were Valentina Tereshkova. Write down how you would feel about:
   (a) going up into space,
   (b) being in orbit,
   (c) coming down again.

2 Do you think other people in space felt the same? How would you feel?

Launch systems

Rocket speeds up to push satellite away from Earth's gravitational pull.

path of the satellite

pull of gravity

The rocket motor is switched off.
The push given by the rocket and the pull of gravity are in balance.

push of rocket

Launching a satellite uses an enormous amount of energy. The rockets have to push against the force of gravity. The higher the satellite is to orbit, the longer the engines have to run. Once the satellite has reached its proper orbit, the engines can be switched off. If the satellite is above the Earth's atmosphere, there will be no air resistance to slow it down. The satellite will stay in the same orbit going at the same speed. If something slows it down, gravity will pull the satellite back to Earth.

Satellite images

Satellites have taken millions of pictures of the Earth's surface. These are used for scientific research, spying, weather forecasts, looking for resources, map making and even searching for the hole in the ozone layer. The examples here show different types of images. What can you see in each one? What could they be used for?

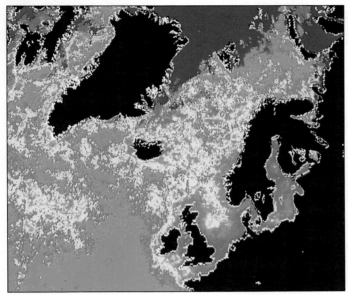

▲ *The colours in this image show the levels of microscopic plant life (phytoplankton) in the North Atlantic. Red is highest, then orange, yellow, green, blue and violet which is lowest. Land is black*

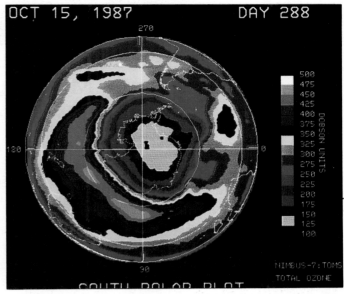

▲ *Ozone 'hole' over the Antarctic (15 Oct 1987). The colours represent amounts of ozone in the atmosphere. Pink is the lowest, then dark blue, pale blue, yellow, red and orange which is the highest*

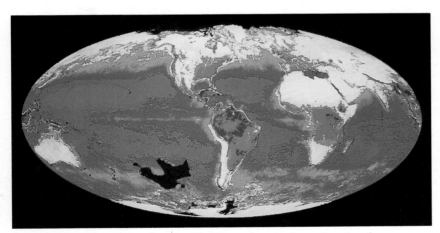

▲ *Plant cover across the world. The colours show levels of chlorophyll (a chemical in all green plants). On land dark green is densest and yellow least dense. In the oceans, red is the most dense then yellow, blue and pink is least dense*

Weather or spy satellites usually have low orbits. You can sometimes see them moving across the night sky as tiny spots of light. Satellites in higher orbits are invisible even with binoculars. Many orbit the Earth at the same speed as the Earth turns, doing one orbit every 24 hours. They are called geostationary satellites. They stay above the same place on the Earth all the time and are used for communications. Radio, television and telephone messages are sent round the world by satellite.

3 Why is a low orbit needed for weather and spy satellites?

4 Why is a high orbit needed for communications satellites?

EXTRAS

1 What would be needed to keep five human beings alive and well for the long flight to Mars (about 4 years)?
- Make a list of the things the space craft would have to do.
- Can you think of any ways these things could be done?

2 Sending people and equipment into space is very expensive. The Apollo project to put a man on the Moon cost £250 billion.
- What are the benefits from this spending?
- What other things would you have spent the money on?

Earth	1 cm = 30 000 km	Moon

The Moon is a satellite of the Earth. It orbits the Earth roughly 400 000 kilometres above the surface. The Moon was formed at the same time as the Earth, about 4.6 billion years ago. It has no atmosphere and so does not support life.

The most beautiful object in the night sky

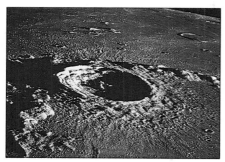

The crater Erastosthenes is 61 km across

The Earth's shadow on the Moon during a partial lunar eclipse

Moonlight

The Moon takes roughly 27 days to complete its orbit of the Earth. It spins on its axis in exactly the same time (27 days). This means that as the Moon orbits the Earth, the same side always faces us.

The surface of the Moon reflects only 7% of the sunlight that falls on it. The brightest full Moon is only a quarter as bright as a candle a metre from you.

Eclipses

Sometimes the Moon passes directly between the Earth and the Sun. The Moon stops some of the Sun's light from reaching Earth. This is a solar eclipse.

Now look at the diagram at the top of the next page. When the Earth passes between the Sun and the Moon, a lunar eclipse occurs. The Earth stops the Sunlight from reaching the Moon's surface.

Lunar eclipse

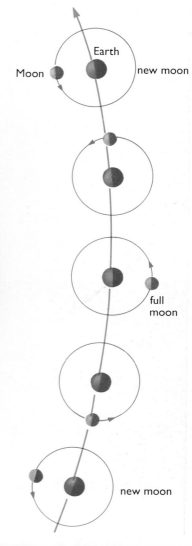

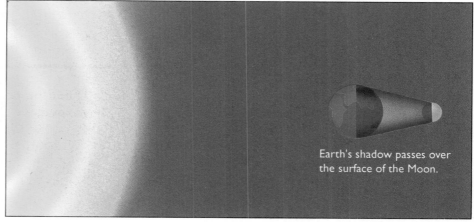

Earth's shadow passes over the surface of the Moon.

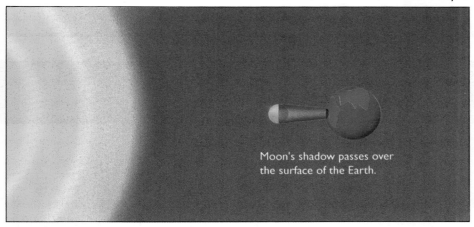

Solar eclipse

Moon's shadow passes over the surface of the Earth.

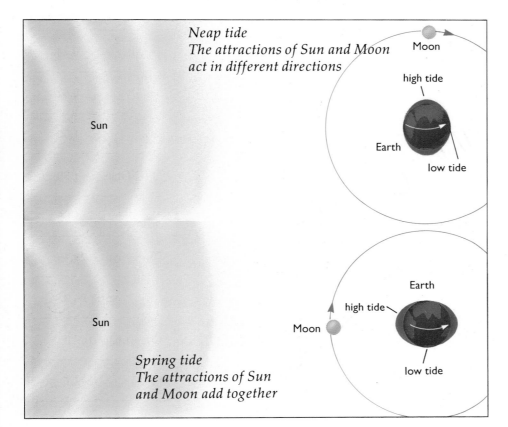

Neap tide
The attractions of Sun and Moon act in different directions

Sun

Moon

high tide

Earth

low tide

Sun

Earth

high tide

Moon

low tide

Spring tide
The attractions of Sun and Moon add together

Tides

The Moon causes tides by pulling on the water in the oceans. The Sun also has an effect on the tides. When the Sun and Moon act together, the tides show a much bigger change. These are called spring tides.

The effect of the Sun on the tides is the same all the year. The effect of the Moon changes as the position of the Moon changes.

1 What keeps the Moon orbiting round the Earth?

2 What stops the Moon from crashing into the Earth?

3 Would an astronaut looking from the Moon's surface always see the same face of the Earth? Explain your answer.

4 Why does the Moon blot out the whole of the Sun even though the Sun is much bigger? Draw a diagram to explain this.

5 Imagine you are an astronaut on the Moon. What would you see of:
– a solar eclipse,
– a lunar eclipse.

6 Which has the bigger effect on the tides – the Sun or the Moon? Explain your answer.

EXTRAS

1 Human beings have walked on the Moon, even though the environment is very hostile.
– How is the environment hostile?
– What does an astronaut's space suit have to do?
– Design a space suit. Use labels to explain its features.
– How is your space suit different from one that would be used by a deep-sea diver?

2 The Moon's surface is covered with meteor craters. Why are there very few meteor craters on the Earth?

Investigating

3 Design and carry out an investigation to find out what controls the size and shape of craters. You could use marbles for meteors and sand for the Moon's surface.

19·4 The planets 1

1 cm = 300 million km

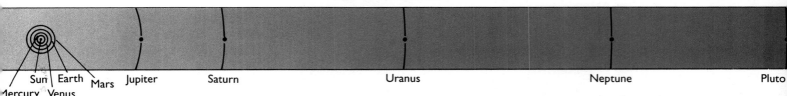

Mercury Venus Sun Earth Mars Jupiter Saturn Uranus Neptune Pluto

Planet	Distance from Sun (million km)	Diameter (km)	Mass (Earth=1)	Number of moons	Gravity (Earth=1)	Density (Water=1)	Average surface temp. (°C)	Time to spin on axis	Time to travel round Sun (years)
Mercury	58	4968	0.05	0	0.4	5.4	510	1416h	0.24
Venus	108	12200	0.8	0	0.9	5.3	480	5832h	0.62
Earth	150	12757	1.0	1	1.0	5.5	15	24h	1.00
Mars	228	6800	0.1	2	0.4	4.0	−50	24h 37min	1.88
Jupiter	779	143600	318	15	2.6	1.3	−250	9h 56min	11.86
Saturn	1427	121000	95	17	1.2	0.7	−180	10h 20min	29.46
Uranus	2670	47000	15	5	1.0	1.6	−200	10h 50min	84.0
Neptune	4496	44600	17	2	1.41	2.2	−220	15h 50min	164.8
Pluto	5906	3000	0.06	1	?	4.5	−240	154h	247.7

Use the table to answer these questions.

1 Which planet has the longest day?
2 Which planet takes the shortest time to travel round the Sun?
3 'The further the planets are from the Sun, the colder they are.' Is this true?
4 Is there a link between the time a planet takes to spin on its axis and the time it takes to go round the Sun?
5 A mass of 1 kg does not weigh the same on Mars as on Earth. Why not? What causes the difference?
6 On Earth, a 1 kg mass weighs 10 N. Use the table to work out what it would weigh on Mars.
7 On which planet would a 1 kg mass be heaviest?

● Make a scale model of the solar system.
– Draw a circle to show the size of each planet. Make sure they are all drawn to the same scale.
– Place the planets on the bench in the right positions.
– The Sun's diameter is 110 times the Earth's diameter. Work out how big a Sun circle would have to be. A calculator may help you.
– The nearest star to Earth is 40 500 000 million kilometres away. Work out how far from the Earth it will be on your scale model.

● Make a computer database about the planets of the solar system. It will be part of an exhibition at a local museum. Make it interesting and easy to use.

Mercury

Mercury is the planet closest to the Sun. The surface temperature of the sunlit side is 510°C, hot enough to melt lead. On the side shielded from the sunlight the temperature drops to −210°C. At this temperature oxygen would be a liquid and nitrogen a solid. Some cliffs on the surface are 2 km high and 16 500 km long.

Many photographs were joined together to give this detailed picture of Mercury, seen by Mariner 10 in 1974

Venus

Venus is the planet nearest to Earth. It has an atmosphere of carbon dioxide. This traps the Sun's heat and keeps the temperature of surface at about 482°C. Clouds of sulphuric acids circle the planet at speeds up to 350 km/h. Radar pictures from the NASA Pioneer spacecraft showed a volcano larger than any on Earth and a mountain higher than Everest.

In the false colour radar image of Venus (above right), blue represents level plains. Green and yellow are mountains

The surface of Venus is photographed by the Russian probe Venera 13 in 1982·

Mars

We are still not sure if there is life on Mars. Experiments carried out by probes that landed there in 1975 did not give a clear answer. Mars has a thin atmosphere which is mainly carbon dioxide. Its surface temperature varies between −21°C and −124°C. The amount of water on Mars is very small and usually frozen underground. The white frost shown in pictures is probably solid carbon dioxide. Strange shapes in the red, rocky deserts of the planet suggest that the planet may once have had large rivers. No one is yet certain if this is true. If it is, where has the water gone?

◀ *Mars. Notice the icecaps at the poles. The ice is a mixture of frozen water and frozen carbon dioxide*

▲ *The first colour photograph of the surface of Mars. Viking I 1976*

Jupiter

Jupiter is the largest planet in the solar system. Its atmosphere is made of clouds of frozen ammonia and water mixed with a lot of other gases. The centre of the planet is a sea of liquid hydrogen and helium at a temperature of about −250°C. This giant planet spins very quickly and has a day of only 9 hours and 55 minutes. Jupiter gives out heat, and this might raise the temperature of one of its moons enough to support life there. This is, however, very unlikely. A weak ring system has been detected round the planet. These rings are like those round Saturn but are much fainter and more difficult to see.

A composite photograph of Jupiter and four of its ▶ *moons*

Saturn

Saturn's rings are the most obvious thing about the planet. They are made up of bits of rock and dust which are often covered in ice. Most of the rocks in the ring are between 3 and 5 metres in diameter. The rings also contain smaller particles. Some of these are not much bigger than specks of dust. Galileo was the first European to see the rings of Saturn. He said the planet appeared to have 'ears'.

The planet itself is made up mainly of oceans of liquid hydrogen.

▲ *Saturn and three of its moons. The small dots at the bottom of the picture are the moons*

The astonishing 'close-up' detail of Saturn's rings photographed from four million kilometres away by Voyager

Uranus

Uranus is the third largest planet in the solar system. It is a gas giant made up of oceans of liquid hydrogen and helium. These oceans are thought to be 9600 kilometres deep with solid hydrogen and helium beneath. At the top of the cloud layer, winds of 700 km/h can be seen pushing clouds at $-200°C$ round the planet. Uranus has a faint system of rings.

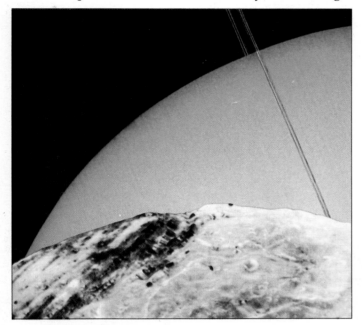

Uranus behind its moon, Miranda

Neptune

Neptune is very like Uranus. It is a gas giant. There are oceans of liquid hydrogen and helium underneath fast-moving gas clouds. Small amounts of methane have been detected on Neptune, and it has a faint ring round it.

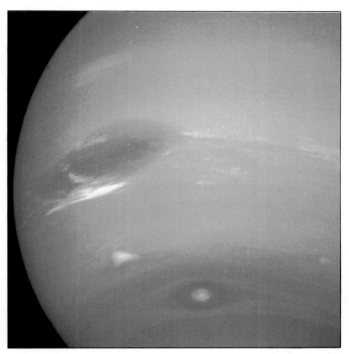

Neptune photographed by Voyager

Pluto

Pluto is the smallest planet in the solar system. It is roughly the size of the Moon. Unlike the Moon it is covered in a crust of solid methane. The temperature of the surface is probably below $-180°C$. Very little is known about Pluto at the moment. We do know it has at least one small moon. This has been called Charon. There may be others.

Artist's impression of Pluto and its moon Charon ▶

EXTRAS

1 Imagine that a planet called Vulcan is on the other side of the Sun, exactly opposite the Earth. The imaginary planet also has the same orbit as the Earth. How could you find out if such a planet exists? What evidence could you collect?

2 (a) Which planet in the solar system is most like Earth? Explain your reasons for making your choice.
(b) What problems would human beings have to solve before they could live there?

Never look directly at the Sun.

The Sun

The Sun is a medium-sized, yellow star 150 million km from us. It provides the energy for all living things on Earth. The energy comes from nuclear fusion. Hydrogen atoms make helium atoms at very high temperatures and pressures, releasing a lot of energy.

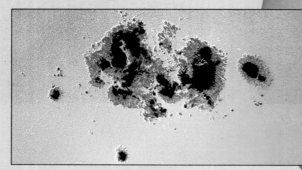

A cluster of sunspots

Sunspots

We can often see darker areas on the Sun's surface. These are called sunspots. Chinese astronomers saw them over 1300 years ago. European scientists ignored them. They thought that the Sun was part of heaven and must be perfect. Sunspots seemed to be blemishes on the face of heaven. They seem to be produced when the Sun is most active.

Sunspots

Solar flares

We can only see solar flares during eclipses or by using a special camera that blanks out the bright central portion of the Sun. They flare without warning into space and give out strong X-rays. This can sometimes disrupt radio waves on Earth.

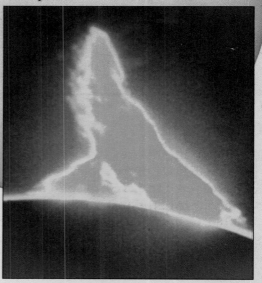

A solar flare photographed by blocking out the light from the Sun's disc

The stars

Stars are energy sources; they produce their own light. Apart from our Sun the nearest star is Alpha Centauri which is about 41 million million kilometres away. The light from the star takes 4.3 years to reach us. The light from the Sun takes just over 8 minutes.

Most of the stars in the sky are so far away that they do not seem to move. However, if you take a photograph on a clear night and leave the camera shutter open for a long time, the stars show up as lines (see the top of the next page). This is caused by the Earth's movement. One star, the Pole Star, does not seem to move. Why is this useful for navigation?

A photograph of star traces taken with a one-hour exposure. The Pole Star is at the centre of the circles.

- Imagine you want to draw a scale map of all the stars. Chose a scale to make Alpha Centauri 5 cm from the Sun. The nearest galaxy to ours would be 100 kilometres away on this scale. The edge of the universe we can see would be 500 million kilometres – just over three times the distance to the Sun.

Mapping the stars

The stars have been named and grouped into constellations. The ancient Greeks named these constellations. Arab astronomers added more names between AD 800 and AD 1000.

People used to think that the stars had an effect on the future. The constellations were supposed to be figures placed in the sky to look after babies born at a particular time. You probably know your own star sign.

The constellation of Orion

Galaxies

Most of the stars we can see without telescopes belong to our galaxy, the Milky Way. It is a group of 100 000 million stars. Our nearest neighbour is the Andromeda galaxy which is 2 million million million kilometres away. The universe is made up of many galaxies. So far, we do not know how many. The furthest star we can see is about 10000 million million million kilometres away.

The Andromeda galaxy. Light takes about 170000 years to travel across the galaxy and about 2.2 million years to reach Earth. Today we see Andromeda as it was about the time of the first humans

EXTRAS

1. Is astrology a useful science or a con trick? Design an investigation to find out. How can you be sure your investigation is completely fair?

2. Why is it impossible to see stars during the daytime?

3. Design a planetarium projector. This should project an image of the constellation Orion on to the ceiling, perhaps your bedroom at home. You could use a tin with holes punched in it and a light inside. Make sure designs you use are safe. What dangers might there be?

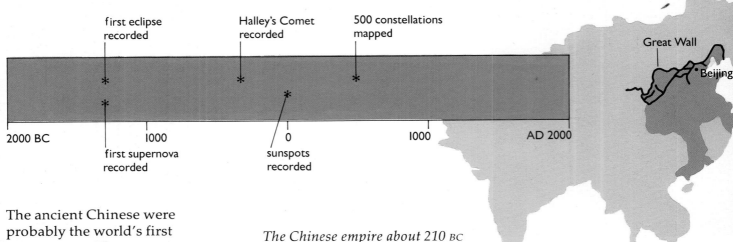

first eclipse recorded

Halley's Comet recorded

500 constellations mapped

Great Wall

Beijing

2000 BC — 1000 — 0 — 1000 — AD 2000

first supernova recorded

sunspots recorded

The Chinese empire about 210 BC

The ancient Chinese were probably the world's first astronomers. They were recording events in the sky over 4000 years ago.

In Europe, sunspots were first recorded by Galileo in 1610. Tycho Brahe and Kepler recorded supernovas in 1572 and 1604. Supernovas are exploding stars. They are very bright for a short time and then fade. By the time the Chinese had catalogued 400 constellations, Europeans had found no more than fifty.

Eclipses	Recorded from 3300 years ago.
Star maps	Over 400 constellations mapped and named by AD 500.
Comets	First recorded 2500 years ago. Halley's comet recorded regularly since 239 BC.
Supernovas	Probably recorded from 3300 years ago. In AD 1054, a very beautiful light was noted. This was probably the supernova explosion that formed the Crab nebula.
Meteor swarms	Recorded over 2700 years ago.
Sunspots	Recorded 2000 years ago.

Measuring instruments

The Chinese did not have telescopes. They made all their observations with the naked eye. It was changes in the skies that mattered to them. They measured the position and angle of the Sun with sundials and shadow sticks.

Astronomers need good clocks. The Chinese developed two types of clock – one for short periods of time and one for longer periods.

Combustion clocks were flat plates of metal or pottery. A channel, cut in the plate, was filled with a material that burned. When lit, the flame passed along the channel like a fuse. As it passed marked points, the exact time could be noted.

Slow burning lines of incense were also used. Different types of incense gave different smells as they burned. In this way, the change in time could be noticed from the change in smell.

Chinese combustion clock

A water clock was used to measure longer periods of time. The illustration shows a water clock from about AD 1090. It was designed by a man called Su Sung. It was important because it had a type of escapement. All the clocks before Su Sung's used smooth movement to mark the passing of time.

An escapement allows the clock's mechanism to move forward in a series of jerks. A short fast movement is followed by a pause and so on. This keeps the clock much more accurate than a smooth movement. Nowadays, all clocks use an escapement. For example, the second hand moves forward instantly, and then waits for a second. It then moves instantly to the next position.

The diagram shows the escapement of Su Sung's clock.

● Write a short paragraph to explain how the escapement works.

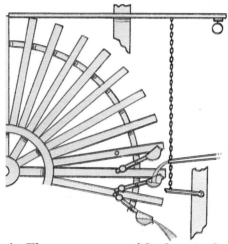

▲ *The escapement of Su Sung's clock*

Su Sung's water clock ▶

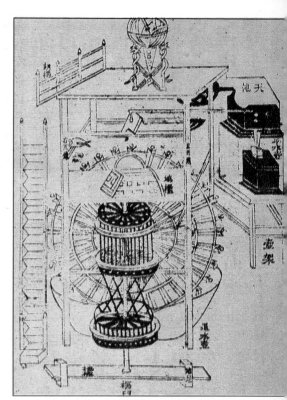

A model of the universe

The Chinese did not worry about whether the Earth went round the Sun or the Sun went round the Earth. It made little difference to them. Their view of the universe had a flat Earth with a dome-shaped sky above it. The stars floated in empty space. This was very different from the European view of a round Earth with ten different skies above it and planets and stars fixed onto the skies.

The purpose of astronomy

Chinese astronomers kept records of the positions of the Sun and Moon and stars and used these to predict future events. This was the main purpose of Chinese astronomy. They did not feel the need to find laws to explain how the planets moved across the sky or whether the Sun went round the Earth. They thought that the heavenly bodies were created for the benefit of human beings and particularly to help the Emperor. He was known as the Son of Heaven and his job was to make sure everything in the empire ran in harmony. The stars and planets were there to guide him. Their 'advice' could not be ignored.

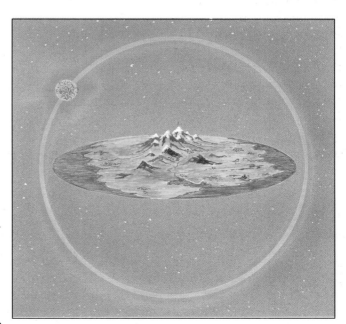

Ancient Chinese view of the universe

EXTRAS

1 When did the Chinese discover supernovas? How long after the Chinese discovered sunspots did Galileo discover them?

2 Build a water clock and test it for accuracy. How accurately can you measure one minute? five minutes?

3 The ancient Chinese were very advanced in their view of the stars. They were much less advanced than the West in their thoughts about the Earth. They viewed the Earth as flat rather than round. What reasons can you find to explain this?

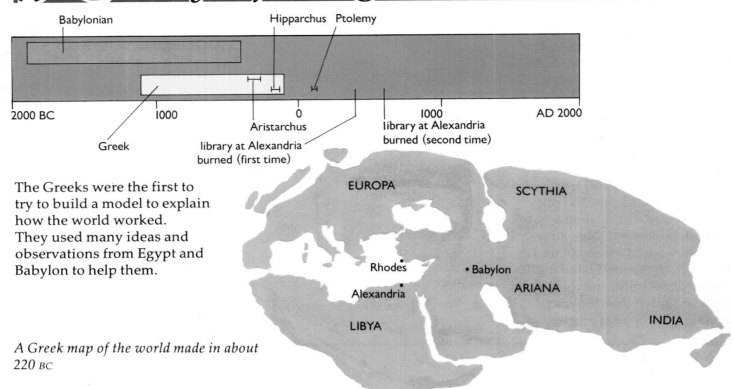

A Greek map of the world made in about 220 BC

The Greeks were the first to try to build a model to explain how the world worked. They used many ideas and observations from Egypt and Babylon to help them.

Aristarchus of Samos
(born about 300 BC)

Aristarchus was a Greek astronomer working in Alexandria. He was the first person to suggest that the Earth moved round the Sun. He even tried to measure the distance to the Sun. His answer was about 8 million kilometres. He also explained that the stars did not seem to move because they were so far away. Again, he was the first person to do this.

Hipparchus of Nicaea
(born about 190 BC)

Hipparchus worked on the island of Rhodes. He made thousands of detailed measurements and compiled a catalogue of over 850 stars. But Hipparchus did not build the model of the universe the Greeks wanted. That job was left to the greatest astronomer of the ancient world, Claudius Ptolemy.

Claudius Ptolemy (born about AD 100)

Ptolemy worked in the city of Alexandria. He used the observations of many earlier astronomers to build the Greek model of the universe. In fact, Ptolemy was thought so important that many of the astronomers whose work he used have been forgotten and their discoveries credited to Ptolemy. Certainly he used Hipparchus' measurements when he wrote his most important book, the *Syntaxis mathematike*.

A round Earth

Ptolemy said that the Earth was 'sensibly spherical'. He put forward evidence to support this idea.
1. Stars do not rise and set at the same time everywhere.
2. An eclipse is seen at different times in different parts of the world.
3. Some stars that can be seen in the North cannot be seen in the South.
4. A ship sailing over the horizon does not just get smaller. The hull disappears first and the top of the mast disappears last.

Communicating

Ptolemy's ideas

● Explain how the evidence above supports Ptolemy's idea. Drawings will help.

1 How could an astronomer who believed the Earth was flat try to explain these observations?

The planets and stars

Ptolemy's ideas about the planets and stars were less accurate. He thought the stars were fixed to a great sphere that surrounded the Earth. The sphere moved round the Earth and made the stars move.

He had trouble explaining the movements of the planets. In the night sky, the planets do not move with the stars all the time. They sometimes make small loops against the star background. Ptolemy explained this by saying that the planets had their own glass-like spheres. These fitted inside the spheres of the stars. Each planet moved in a circle across the surface of these moving spheres.

The Earth was at the very centre of the star sphere and did not move. The spheres were perfectly round because the heavens were the home of the gods and everything about them must be perfect. The Greeks regarded a circle and a sphere as perfect shapes. Ptolemy again produced evidence to support his ideas.

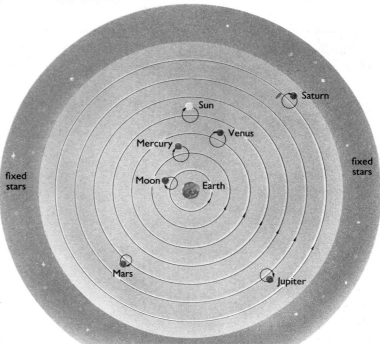

Ptolemy's picture of the universe

1. Heavy objects fall towards the Earth in straight lines. Aristotle, a Greek philosopher from nearly 500 years earlier insisted that heavy things always 'fell towards the centre'. The Earth must be the centre or things would fall away from it.

2. If the solid Earth turned from west to east then the winds would always blow from east to west. Obviously this did not happen.

■2 How would a modern astronomer explain these points? (It might help to draw some diagrams.)

Ptolemy the thinker

Ptolemy was a great thinker but perhaps not such a great experimenter. Some people have suggested that many of his observations belonged to Hipparchus. Sometimes Ptolemy confirms data from Hipparchus that we know was wrong. It also seems possible he made up some observations to support his own ideas. However, he did produce a model that explained many of the observations made by astronomers. The Greeks clearly wanted to believe him.

The burning of the library

The Christians thought Ptolemy's theory was the result of an older, pagan tradition. They felt it was wrong and dangerous because it contradicted the Bible. Much of the library of the University of Alexandria (where Ptolemy had worked) was destroyed by fire about AD 400. Many valuable books were lost because (some said) the Christians did not try very hard to put the fire out.

When the Arabs took over the area 200 years later, they completed the job. They burned many of the remaining books to heat the public baths in the city. This time, people felt that many Greek books disagreed with the Koran (the Muslim holy book). Fortunately some of Ptolemy's works survived. They were translated into Arabic and called the 'almagest'.

EXTRAS

1 Make a model of Ptolemy's universe. Try to make a two-dimensional model showing the orbits of the stars and of one planet round the Earth. You could use cardboard shapes and pins to mark the centres of the spheres.

2 What did the ancient Greeks try to do that the Chinese did not? Why do you think this was an important difference?

The ancient Greeks and Chinese both thought that the universe does not change. They believed it had remained the same since it was created. This view has only changed in the last 100 years.

The 'big bang'

Here is one modern view of the life story of our universe.

1 The universe began as a tiny lump of matter. It was infinitely small and infinitely hot. Common-sense laws of physics did not apply to the matter in the lump.

2 The dot exploded in 'the big bang'. It reached enormous temperatures. A second later it had cooled to a temperature of 10 000 million °C. This was still too hot for atoms to hold together.

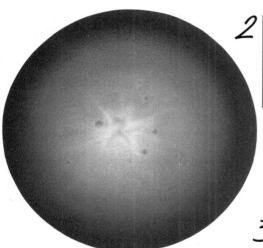

3 Another 100 seconds and the temperature was down to 1000 million °C. This is as hot as the centre of the hottest stars. The elements hydrogen and helium formed.

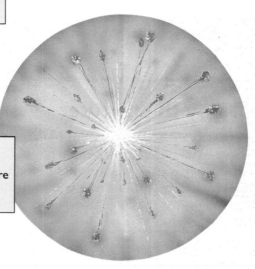

4

A few hours later, hydrogen and helium production stopped. The universe continued getting bigger and cooler for millions of years.

5

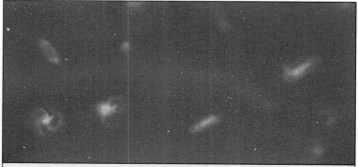

Eventually the temperature dropped to only a few thousand degrees Celsius. Other atoms started to form. In some areas there would be more atoms than in others. The gravitational pull of these denser areas attracted more atoms. Unbalanced forces often caused these collection of bits to start to spin; giant spinning galaxies were formed.

6 The stars started to build new elements as atoms crashed into each other. Eventually some ran out of hydrogen and helium fuel. The result was a giant explosion called a supernova. This threw heavier elements out into space. Some would make more stars; some would condense into planets.

7 The Earth began as a hot ball of debris from a supernova. The cooling rocks gave out gases. Some very primitive life forms managed to evolve in the poisonous atmosphere of methane and ammonia. Over millions of years, the living things on the planet changed the atmosphere to give its present mixture of oxygen and nitrogen.

The universe is still expanding. At some point in the future it may slow down and stop. If that happens, the forces of gravity could start pulling it all back together again. The stars and galaxies would rush together to make an infinitely small, infinitely hot ball. This is known as 'the big crunch'. After that, we cannot guess what might happen . . .

Albert Einstein
(1879 – 1955)

A poet once said about Newton:
> Nature and Nature's laws lay hid in night:
> God said, 'Let Newton be!' and all was light.

A more modern poet added:
> The Devil then, with heave and ho,
> Said, 'Let Einstein be!' and restored the status quo.

Newton tried to describe the universe with simple, common-sense laws. Einstein showed this was not possible. His theories show that time does not pass at the same speed everywhere. It goes more slowly on a fast-moving rocket than on the ground. Also a rocket travelling near the speed of light has more mass than one that is not moving. He predicted black holes – places where gravity is so strong that everything, including light, is trapped and nothing can escape. Einstein was the greatest scientist of the 20th century and his ideas form the basis of much of modern physics.

Albert Einstein himself was a strange mixture. He was a pacifist who helped develop the atomic bomb, a Jew who did not believe in God and a politician who turned down the offer of the presidency of Israel.

During the First World War he campaigned against the waste of human lives. He encouraged people not to join the army and was involved in strikes and demonstrations. People round him lost sympathy with him. In 1933, the Nazis came to power in Germany while Einstein was lecturing in the United States. He said he would never return to Germany. The Nazis raided his house, confiscated his bank account and publicly burned his books.

During the war, he felt he had to renounce his pacifist views. In a letter to President Franklin Roosevelt, he insisted the allies should build an atomic bomb before the Nazis did. The success of the Manhattan Project (the project to build the first atomic bomb) horrified him. He spent the rest of his life seeking to control the new weapons his work had made possible. After seeing the effects of the atomic bomb, he said 'If I had known it would have led to this, I would have become a watchmaker.'

Index